Stir It Up

Stir Up the Gift of God

Dag Heward-Mills

Parchment House

Unless otherwise stated, all Scripture quotations are taken from the King James Version of the Bible.

Stir It Up
Stir Up the Gift of God

Published by Parchment House 2022
1st Printing 2022

Find out more about Dag Heward-Mills
Healing Jesus Campaign
Write to: evangelist@daghewardmills.org
Website: www.daghewardmills.org
Facebook: Dag Heward-Mills
Twitter: @EvangelistDag

ISBN: 978-1-64330-516-5

Contents

CHAPTER 1

Stir Up the Gift of God

Wherefore I put thee in remembrance that thou STIR UP THE GIFT OF GOD, which is in thee by the putting on of my hands.

2 Timothy 1:6

You are anointed! You are called by God! You have the gift of God! Many things are lying dormant in you. The world is waiting for you to manifest the power of the Holy Spirit.

It is important that you stir up the great things that are already in you. Many people will be saved. Many people will be healed. Many people will be blessed when the gift of God in you is fully stirred up into action.

Unfortunately, many people live and die without using their gifts. Many gifted people live their lives without stirring up their gifts. This book is about how to stir up your gift.

After reading this book, you will become a surprise to the world! Many will be amazed at the greatness of the gift of God in you.

1. Stir Up the Lion.

I can best describe you as a great lion full of power and glory. You are a capable lion with muscles, strong teeth and a strong bite who is lying down quietly. Your potential is huge. Notice how Israel is described as a lion waiting to be stirred up.

> God brought him forth out of Egypt; he hath as it were the strength of an unicorn: he shall eat up the nations his enemies, and shall break their bones, and pierce them through with his arrows. HE COUCHED, HE LAY DOWN AS A LION, AND AS A GREAT LION: WHO SHALL STIR HIM UP? Blessed is he that blesseth thee, and cursed is he that curseth thee.
>
> Numbers 24:8-9

When you are released into the world, and when your gift is stirred up, many will be saved and changed. You are going to affect the world for Jesus Christ.

2. Stir Up the Eagle.

You are like an eagle in a nest that has never flown. All you know is life in the nest. As an eagle, you have great potential. You can fly long distances. You can hunt and kill four-legged animals. You can eat fish, reptiles, mammals and even other birds. You are very powerful. Indeed, you are the most powerful bird. Yet you need to be stirred up otherwise your greatness will never be known. Notice how Israel is described as an eagle that needs to be stirred up to manifest itself.

> For the LORD'S portion is his people; Jacob is the lot of his inheritance.
>
> He found him in a desert land, and in the waste howling wilderness; he led him about, he instructed him, he kept him as the apple of his eye.
>
> AS AN EAGLE STIRRETH UP HER NEST, FLUTTERETH OVER HER YOUNG, SPREADETH ABROAD HER WINGS, TAKETH THEM, BEARETH THEM ON HER WINGS:
>
> So the LORD alone did lead him, and there was no strange god with him.
>
> He made him ride on the high places of the earth, that he might eat the increase of the fields; and he made him to suck honey out of the rock, and oil out of the flinty rock;
>
> Deuteronomy 32:9-13

As you read this book, your great capabilities and gifts are going to be seen. You will fly for long distances along the contours of this earth. Eagles are not troubled by the contours of this earth. Your ministry will not be affected by the highs and lows of life on earth. The financial ups and downs will not control or determine your output.

You are described prophetically as an eagle that can soar to great heights and cover great distances. You are going to the heights of ministry! You are going to cover much ground in a short while! Many will be amazed by the heights that you will achieve in ministry as you allow the gift of God in you to be stirred up.

It is amazing what both a lion and an eagle can achieve. A lion is king of the beasts on the earth and the eagle reigns supreme in the air! Yet, both of these need stirring up! Beginning from today, your ministry will assume enormous proportions and great heights. By the stirring up of your gifts you will become the lion you are born to be. By the stirring up of your gifts you will become the eagle you are born to be.

3. Stir up Supernatural Gifts.

Wherefore I put thee in remembrance that thou STIR UP THE GIFT OF GOD, which is in thee by the putting on of my hands.

2 Timothy 1:6

You must stir up the anointing that is in you. You must stir up the gift that is in you. Without stirring up the gift of God, the manifestations will not happen. All through the ministry of Jesus you will see how He stirred up the gift and the anointing of the Holy Spirit. Jesus Christ performed the greatest miracles ever seen by mankind. Jesus operated and manifested the greatest anointing ever seen by human beings.

How did He do it? How did He stir up the anointing that had been given to Him by God? Remember that Jesus put aside His divinity and took on the form of a man. He therefore needed to be anointed and empowered just like every other human being needs to be.

4. Stir up the Anointing.

After being anointed, Jesus needed to stir up the anointing. The anointing on Him could be likened to a sleeping lion that needed to be stirred up into action. "He couched, he lay down as a lion, and as a great lion: who shall stir him up?" (Numbers

4

24:9) The anointing on Jesus could also be likened to an eagle that could be stirred up to fly at the highest altitudes. "As an eagle stirreth up her nest, fluttereth over her young, spreadeth abroad her wings, taketh them, beareth them on her wings..." (Deuteronomy 32:11).

You must see how the anointing is stirred up in the ministry of Jesus and stir up the anointing in yourself. You must understand what stirs up the anointing by looking at the ministry of Jesus. A closer look at the miracles of Jesus will reveal what stirred up the anointing in every single power encounter.

5. Stir Up the Works.

I MUST WORK THE WORKS of him that sent me, while it is day: the night cometh, when no man can work.

John 9:4

Jesus said He would work the works of God. The works of God are worked out by doing things. The great works that Jesus did had the characteristic of being worked out. Jesus did not just sit and wait for things to happen. He worked the works of the Father. There are great works in you! There are sermons you must preach! There are buildings you must build! There are churches you must plant! There are miracles you must do. None of these will happen naturally. None of these will happen just because you are anointed. You must stir up the works of God.

6. Stir Up the Miracles.

But the manifestation of the Spirit is given to every man to profit withal. For to one is given by the Spirit the word of wisdom; to another the word of knowledge by the same Spirit; To another faith by the same Spirit; to another the gifts of healing by the same Spirit; To another the WORKING OF MIRACLES; to another prophecy; to another discerning of spirits; to another divers kinds of tongues; to another the interpretation of tongues: But all these worketh that one and the selfsame Spirit, dividing to every man severally as he will.

1 Corinthians 12:7-11

Indeed, you don't wait for miracles, you work miracles!

Stir up the supernatural part of you or it will not be stirred up.

Stir up the gift of God otherwise it will remain dormant.

7. Stir up the Power.

Jesus stirred up the power of God in several different ways. Let us look at the methods by which Jesus stirred up the anointing. You must use these same methods in your ministry and you will receive the same results that Jesus did.

There are things that you must do that will stir up the power of God. There are steps that you can take that will cause the anointing to be stirred up in you. There are also things that people can do that will stir up the anointed and his powerful anointing.

Obedience stirs up the power of God!

Doing what the Father does stirs up the gifts of God!

Pleasing God stirs up the power of God!

Stir up miracle power by setting things in order!

Being sensitive stirs up the anointing.

Faith stirs up the power of God.

Pleading with God stirs up the power of God.

Humility stirs up the anointing.

Compassion stirs up the power.

Travelling stirs up the anointing.

Praying for mercy stirs up the anointing.

Honour stirs up the anointing.

Pressing through stirs up the anointing.

Persistence stirs up the power of God.

Breaking tradition stirs up the anointing.

Following prophetic directions stirs up the prophetic anointing.

All these different things will change your power levels. In this book, you will learn how to stir up the power of God in your life and ministry.

Indeed, many things will not work unless they are stirred up. All through the Bible you will see the need to stir up gifts, stir up people, stir up ideas and stir up gifted people.

CHAPTER 2

Stir Up Many Things

And the LORD stirred up the spirit of Zerubbabel the son of Shealtiel, governor of Judah, and the spirit of Joshua the son of Josedech, the high priest, and the spirit of all the remnant of the people; and they came and did work in the house of the LORD of hosts, their God...

Hagai 1:14

1. STIR UP PEOPLE TO GIVE.

If people are not stirred up, they will not give to support the vision. Some pastors do not know why they do not have enough money. They have not learnt how to stir people up to give. Moses was asked to receive an offering from willing people. People become willing to give when the Holy Spirit stirs them up to give. They give willingly when they are stirred up by their leader. You must develop the art of stirring up the congregation to give and to support the work of God. You must watch out for signs that people are stirred up to give.

> And Moses spake unto all the congregation of the children of Israel, saying, This is the thing which the LORD commanded, saying, Take ye from among you an offering unto the LORD: whosoever is of a willing heart, let him bring it, an offering of the LORD; gold, and silver, and brass …
>
> AND THEY CAME, EVERY ONE WHOSE HEART STIRRED HIM UP, AND EVERY ONE WHOM HIS SPIRIT MADE WILLING, AND THEY BROUGHT THE LORD'S OFFERING TO THE WORK OF THE TABERNACLE OF THE CONGREGATION, and for all his service, and for the holy garments. And they came, both men and women, as many as were willing hearted, and brought bracelets, and earrings, and rings, and tablets, all jewels of gold: and every man that offered offered an offering of gold unto the LORD.
>
> Exodus 35: 4-5, 21-22

2. A LEADER MUST STIR UP THE PEOPLE TO USE THEIR SKILLS FOR GOD.

People need to be stirred up to use their skills. There are many gifted people around you. Most of them will live and die without showing you what they can really do. If you stir them up, you will find out that you have the most talented people around you. There are women who can do amazing things if you stir them up and give them work.

I have seen many women released in the ministry who can do amazing things because they have been stirred up to serve the Lord. "And all the women that were wise hearted did spin with their hands, and brought that which they had spun, both of blue, and of purple, and of scarlet, and of fine linen. And ALL THE WOMEN WHOSE HEART STIRRED THEM UP IN WISDOM SPUN GOATS' HAIR" (Exodus 35:25-26).

There are many men, like Bezaleel, who can do wonders if they are released to serve God. Bezaleel was used greatly by God. "Then wrought Bezaleel and Aholiab, and every wise hearted man, in whom the LORD put wisdom and understanding to know how to work all manner of work for the service of the sanctuary, according to all that the LORD had commanded. And Moses called Bezaleel and Aholiab, and every wise hearted man, in whose heart the LORD had put wisdom, EVEN EVERY ONE WHOSE HEART STIRRED HIM UP TO COME UNTO THE WORK TO DO IT:" (Exodus 36:1-2). Even though Bezaleel and Aholiab had wisdom and skill, they still needed to be stirred up to serve the Lord.

3. STIR UP YOURSELF TO TAKE HOLD OF GOD.

Pastors must stir themselves up to take hold of God. Pastors must stir up the people to love God, to follow God and to serve God. If the leader does not encourage the people and stir them up, people will not serve the Lord. When a pastor stirs up the people, they will be stirred to take hold of God themselves.

But we are all as an unclean thing, and all our righteousnesses are as filthy rags; and we all do fade as a leaf; and our iniquities, like the wind, have taken us away. AND THERE IS NONE THAT CALLETH UPON THY NAME, THAT STIRRETH UP HIMSELF TO TAKE

HOLD OF THEE: for thou hast hid thy face from us, and hast consumed us, because of our iniquities.

Isaiah 64:6-7

4. STIR YOURSELF UP TO LOVE.

People need to be stirred up to love. We often hear the exhortation, "Husbands, love your wives." This is important because without the exhortation, there will be very little love. Wives are also exhorted to love their husbands. Love must be stirred up. If love is not stirred up, there will be very little love. Many people have love but because it is not stirred up they seem to be loveless and emotionless. It is time to stir up love. Every pastor must attempt to stir up love in the congregation.

I charge you, O ye daughters of Jerusalem, by the roes, and by the hinds of the field, that YE STIR NOT UP, NOR AWAKE MY LOVE, till he please.

Song of Solomon 2:7

I charge you, O ye daughters of Jerusalem, by the roes, and by the hinds of the field, that YE STIR NOT UP, NOR AWAKE MY LOVE, till he please.

Song of Solomon 3:5

5. STIR UP PEOPLE TO BUILD THE CHURCH.

People need to be stirred up to build the church of God. The congregation is made of sheep that need to be led and guided along the way. If you stir them up, they would love to get involved in building the church. A pastor must teach and lead by example until people take joy in building the house of God.

And THE LORD STIRRED UP THE SPIRIT OF ZERUBBABEL the son of Shealtiel, governor of Judah, and the spirit of Joshua the son of Josedech, the high priest, and the spirit of all the remnant of the people; and

11

THEY CAME AND DID WORK IN THE HOUSE OF
THE LORD OF HOSTS, THEIR GOD,

Haggai 1:14

6. STIR UP AGAINST IDOLATRY.

Now while Paul waited for them at Athens, HIS SPIRIT
WAS STIRRED IN HIM, WHEN HE SAW THE CITY
WHOLLY GIVEN TO IDOLATRY.

Acts 17:16

People need to be stirred up against idolatry. One of the
greatest spiritual provocations of all is idolatry. If you took the
picture of a snake or a crab and framed it and wrote the name of
a presi-dent of your country under it, would it not be considered
an insult? This is what you do when you take a goat, an antelope,
a snake, a river or any piece of wood and say that it is your
creator. It is one of the greatest provocations against God.

7. STIR UP YOUR MEMORY.

Yea, I think it meet, as long as I am in this tabernacle, TO
STIR YOU UP BY PUTTING YOU IN REMEMBRANCE;

2 Peter 1:13

People's memories need to be stirred up. I wrote a book called
"Those Who Forget." Many people forget important things. Life
is all about remembering the right things at the right time. If you
know something but do not remember it during your exams, you
will still fail. Failure is because people do not remember what
they should remember when they should remember it.

All over the world things are done to make people remember.
Plaques, monuments, posters, gravestones, memorials and statues
are all efforts to make people remember things. Rebellious and
disloyal people are the most forgetful of all.

They cannot remember that something good was done for
them. Because they do not remember, they become failures and

losers. I predict that all those who live their lives forgetting all
that has been done for them will become destitute. They will beg
for bread and there will be none to show mercy to them.

8. STIR UP YOUR MIND.

This second epistle, beloved, I now write unto you; IN
BOTH WHICH I STIR UP YOUR PURE MINDS by way
of remembrance:

2 Peter 3:1

People's minds need to be stirred up. It is important to stir
your mind up so that you think properly. Many people have
great minds but these minds are not stirred up to think proper
thoughts. You can stir up somebody's mind by making him
think and analyse. Making people remember things stirs up
their mind.

Sometimes people live in sin and do not realize how far they
have gone. When you stir up their pure minds by way of analysis
or remembrance, they start to think correctly. Demons work by
imparting thoughts to our minds. Demon activity is why people
think wrongly. This is why we have to cast down imaginations
of the wrong things. You must think on the right things.

Your mind has the capacity to think and to reason. God gave
you this ability. A little bit of thinking and a little bit of analysis
will do you a lot of good. Many murderers do not think deeply
about what they are doing.

I read about a young pastor who murdered his even younger
wife in broad daylight. He shot her several times in broad
daylight. He must have been very upset with his wife. It is not
unusual for a man to be upset with his wife but a bit of thinking
would have saved him from destroying two lives.

When I read the story, I thought to myself, "Does this young
man realize that he is condemning himself to a life of misery
behind bars?" Does he realize that he will never be free again?

Does he realize that he is sinning before God by committing murder? A little thinking and a little analysis would have helped this young man to avoid destroying his life. Perhaps, his emotions were stirred up but his mind was not stirred up. Many rebellious people have their emotions stirred up but their minds are not working.

There was a brother who gave himself to drinking alcohol. He would come home drunk every day. One day his pastor asked him, "Why are you drinking so much?" He said he drank to forget about his wife and the troubles that she brought to him. This young man was not thinking clearly because he had developed an unusual side effect from the alcohol – he was seeing everything double! Now, every time he came home, he saw two wives! Indeed, his problems doubled when he drank!

CHAPTER 3

Stir Up Devils and Cast Them Out!

And they came over unto the other side of the sea, into the country of the Gadarenes. And when he was come out of the ship, immediately there met him out of the tombs a man with an unclean spirit, Who had his dwelling among the tombs; and no man could bind him, no, not with chains: Because that he had been often bound with fetters and chains, and the chains had been plucked asunder by him, and the fetters broken in pieces: neither could any man tame him.

And always, night and day, he was in the mountains, and in the tombs, crying, and cutting himself with stones.

But when he saw Jesus afar off, he ran and worshipped him, And cried with a loud voice, and said, what have I to do with thee, Jesus, thou Son of the most high God? I adjure thee by God, that thou torment me not. For he said unto him, Come out of the man, thou unclean spirit.

And he asked him, What is thy name? And he answered, saying, my name is Legion: for we are many.

And he besought him much that he would not send them away out of the country.

Now there was there nigh unto the mountains a great herd of swine feeding.

And all the devils besought him, saying, Send us into the swine, that we may enter into them. And forthwith Jesus gave them leave. And the unclean spirits went out, and entered into the swine: and the herd ran violently down a steep place into the sea, (they were about two thousand;) and were choked in the sea.

And they that fed the swine fled, and told it in the city, and in the country. And they went out to see what it was that was done.

And they come to Jesus, and see him that was possessed with the devil, and had the legion, sitting, and clothed, and in his right mind: and they were afraid.

Mark 5:1-15

Keys to Stirring Up the Power of God

1. **Stirring by eagerness:** Eagerness stirs up the power of God. Keenness, enthusiasm, excitement, readiness and zeal all stir up the power of God. As soon as Jesus encountered the mad man, he ran and worshipped Jesus: "But when he saw Jesus afar off, he ran and worshipped him" (Mark 5:6).

The excitement of this man when he saw Jesus, stirred up the power of God. Everyone is revived when he has an exciting, keen and enthusiastic person to minister to. Men are always in search of an exciting, ready, enthusiastic and eager woman to relate with. Equally, God is in search of such characteristics. It stirs up the power of God. Jesus performed one of the greatest miracles of His entire ministry because He encountered such a person. Even though the man was mad, he was keen and enthusiastic, just on seeing Jesus. There are some congregations that are made up of dull, unexciting and tired-looking faces. These congregations do not stir up the power of God. I once attended a service where I encountered happy, excited, enthusiastic young people. I preached for two and a half hours without noticing how long I had preached.

One day, someone said to me, "Your sermons are now two and half hours long on the podcast." I argued and said it was impossible.

"I preach for forty-five minutes," I said, but the person was right. I had indeed been preaching for more than two hours every Sunday.

The teaching anointing and the pastoral anointing had been stirred up by the presence of a newer, younger and more eager congregation. This is the reason why ministers must travel and not stay in one location. Each time a minister moves, he encounters a more enthusiastic and exciting congregation. The gift of God is always stirred up by the keenness and enthusiasm of the recipients.

2. **Stirring by rejecting evil:** Challenging evil stirs up the power of God. Expelling evil! Demanding that evil things depart! Rejecting evil releases the power of God! Jesus rejected the evil spirits that were in the man. He refused to allow the evil spirits to be there. "For he said unto him, Come out of the man, thou unclean spirit" (Mark 5:8).

3. **Stirring by asking questions:** Asking questions stirs up the power of God. Jesus asked the demon an important question. "And he asked him, 'What is thy name?' And he answered, saying, 'My name is Legion: for we are many'" (Mark 5:9). Your failure to ask about certain details reveals your lack of interest and apathy about the ministry. Jesus got to know the name and number of His enemies that were present. There are things you must ask many questions about. Know your enemy and in a hundred battles you will never be defeated!

4. **Stirring by wisdom:** The wisdom of God stirs up the anointing. Jesus allowed the demons to go into the pigs. Some people may consider that a compromise. Through this action of Jesus, somebody's pig farm of a two thousand pigs was destroyed. Indeed, someone had to pay a great price and lose a lot of money for these demons to leave the man and set him free.

Did Jesus allow evil to prevail? Certainly not! Did Jesus allow the devils to do whatever they wanted? Certainly not! Jesus gained the upper hand over the devils by letting them enter the pigs. It seemed as though evil prevailed but ultimately the man was set free. The goal was to set the man free from evil powers.

When Jesus went to the cross, it may seem as though murderers, liars, thieves and wicked men had triumphed over good. It seemed as though treachery, deception and evil had prevailed and had its way. But that was the wisdom of God in action. Through the cross (the apparent defeat of Jesus and His ministry), salvation came to the whole world. You and I are saved through the blood of Jesus. Today, millions of people are saved from the clutches of devils. This has happened just because Jesus seemed to allow devils to triumph over Him, only to destroy their strong grip over the human race.

CHAPTER 4

Stir Up Supplies

And the third day there was A MARRIAGE IN CANA OF GALILEE; and the mother of Jesus was there: And both Jesus was called, and his disciples, to the marriage. And when they wanted wine, the mother of Jesus saith unto him, They have no wine. Jesus saith unto her, Woman, what have I to do with thee? mine hour is not yet come.

HIS MOTHER SAITH UNTO THE SERVANTS, WHATSOEVER HE SAITH UNTO YOU, DO IT. And there were set there six waterpots of stone, after the manner of the purifying of the Jews, containing two or three firkins apiece.

Jesus saith unto them, Fill the waterpots with water. And they filled them up to the brim. And he saith unto them, Draw out now, and bear unto the governor of the feast. And they bare it. When the ruler of the feast had tasted the water that was made wine, and knew not whence it was:(but the servants which drew the water knew;) the governor of the feast called the bridegroom, And saith unto him, Every man at the beginning doth set forth good wine; and when men have well drunk, then that which is worse: but thou hast kept the good wine until now.

John 2:1-10

1. Stir up ABUNDANCE by obedience.

The miracle of turning water into wine reveals the power of obedience to release the supernatural power of provision. The power of God was stirred up to deliver them from embarrassment.

The miracle in Cana of Galilee saw water being turned into wine. This miracle happened in front of many guests. Jesus' mother knew that her son was anointed. At least she knew that He was an unusual child and that He had some powers that she had not given to Him.

Even though Jesus' mother did not fully understand her son, she knew that there was something they would do that would stir up His "magical" powers. "His mother saith unto the servants, whatsoever he saith unto you, do it" (John 2:5). In other words, Jesus' mother was telling the servants to be a hundred per cent obedient to Jesus. If they were obedient and followed all that He said to the letter, she knew that miracle power would be stirred up. Just obey everything He says and you will see the power of God. Indeed, obedience is the master key to stirring up the power of God.

When you walk in obedience, the power of God begins to flow. Many things that look impossible become possible when you walk in obedience to God's command. Jesus said very clearly: He that keeps my commandments will experience a manifestation of God's love and God's presence. "He that hath my commandments, and keepeth them, he it is that loveth me: and he that loveth me shall be loved of my Father, and I will love him, and will manifest myself to him" (John 14:21).

2. Stir up MANIFESTATIONS by obedience.

Manifestations will happen to those who love God. Those who love God are those who are obedient. Obedience will stir up the power of God like nothing else.

22

Make sure that you hear from God and make sure that you know His will. If you are sure that you have heard from God, obeying Him and implementing His will, will stir up the power of God. Whatever He says to you, do it!

Jesus is the only person we know who was born of a virgin. Isaac was not born of a virgin, Sarah. When Abraham was ninety years old, he received instructions from God to have a child in his old age. His wife was also barren and old. She needed a miracle of healing and a miracle of rejuvenation. Abraham obeyed God in doing what he could to make his wife pregnant at that old age. Through his obedience, miracle power flowed into Abraham and Sarah's life and baby Isaac was conceived and born in nine months.

If you think deeply about the difficulties and the barriers that stood before Abraham, you will agree with me that the power of God had really moved in their lives to give birth to Isaac.

3. Stir up MIRACLES by obedience.

In the same way, Zacharias saw the angel of God in his old age. He and his wife, Elizabeth, received power to give birth to a child in their old age. "And, behold, thy cousin Elisabeth, she hath also conceived a son in her old age: and this is the sixth month with her, who was called barren" (Luke 1:36). Having a child in your old age is a real miracle because the reproductive part of the body is completely shut down after a certain age.

The power of God flowed into my life as I obeyed the Lord in starting a church. It is that power that caused the church to grow. If God had not sent me to start a church, I would not be obeying Him and there would be no power. The gift of God is stirred up when you are walking in obedience. Whatever He says to you, do it!

When the Lord sent me to have crusades, I stirred up the power of God by obeying Him. I had a clear vision in which the Lord said I should pray for the sick. Each time I pray for the sick on the crusade platform, I am obeying what the Lord told me to do and each time the power of God is stirred up into action. That is how to stir up the healing anointing.

Are you wondering why the power of God does not seem to be stirred up and activated in your life? Miracle power and supernatural interventions are stirred up simply by acts of obedience. Remember to obey God in the big things as well as in the little things.

In order to release such power that could turn water into wine, the servants had to obey Jesus' simple instructions. Are you averse to simple instructions? Do you consider certain things too simple or too trivial? I often notice how people despise little instructions they are given. Their faces give them away. I can tell they are not impressed.

Are you too proud to listen to instructions about minor things? "Jesus saith unto them, Fill the waterpots with water. And they filled them up to the brim. And he saith unto them, Draw out now, and bear unto the governor of the feast. And they bare it" (John 2:7-8).

When you obey God's instructions to the letter, you will stir up the power of God. You will see the power of God in every aspect of your life. It is the little things that require more faith and more obedience and it is often those little things that release a lot of power.

Stir up the power that leads to all financial provision! Begin to stir up the power of God by your obedience. It takes the power of God to experience financial provision as well as provision of all that you need. Have you wondered why you lack so many things? Have you wondered why you never have enough money? The power of supernatural provision will come into your life when you are obedient!

CHAPTER 5

Stir Up Overdue Miracles

Now there is at Jerusalem by the sheep market a pool, which is called in the Hebrew tongue Bethesda, having five porches.

In these lay a great multitude of impotent folk, of blind, halt, withered, waiting for the moving of the water.

For an angel went down at a certain season into the pool, and troubled the water: whosoever then first after the troubling of the water stepped in was made whole of whatsoever disease he had.

And a certain man was there, which had an infirmity thirty and eight years.

WHEN JESUS SAW HIM LIE, AND KNEW THAT HE HAD BEEN NOW A LONG TIME IN THAT CASE, HE SAITH UNTO HIM, WILT THOU BE MADE WHOLE?

The impotent man answered him, Sir, I have no man, when the water is troubled, to put me into the pool: but while I am coming, another steppeth down before me.

Jesus saith unto him, Rise, take up thy bed, and walk.

And immediately the man was made whole, and took up his bed, and walked: and on the same day was the Sabbath.

The Jews therefore said unto him that was cured, it is the Sabbath day: it is not lawful for thee to carry thy bed.

He answered them, He that made me whole, the same said unto me, Take up thy bed, and walk.

Then asked they him, What man is that which said unto thee, Take up thy bed, and walk? And he that was healed wist not who it was: for Jesus had conveyed himself away, a multitude being in that place.

John 5:2-13

1. Stir it up by being faithful.

Some miracles are overdue. Some miracles have taken a long time to arrive. The story of the man by the Pool of Bethesda is an example of an overdue miracle. Today marks the end of the wait for your overdue miracles.

The story of the healing by the Pool of Bethesda also illustrates the effects of not stirring up the gift of God with faith, aggression and speed. This man had been lying by the pool for thirty-eight years. Thirty-eight years is a very long time to wait for a miracle.

God's power can work in your life even when you do not stir it up through faith, aggression and speed. People who do not use the necessary aggression, speed and faith also have the power of God working in their lives. Faithfulness and constantness is a powerful trait that brings about the manifestation of the power of God.

There are times you have to appoint people not because of their dynamism, their aggression or even their obedience. There are times you must look only at their faithfulness, constantness and persistence in the things of God. Perhaps the Lord looked on the thirty-eight years of this man's unwavering presence and decided to reward him.

Look around you and see the faithful people who have served without shifting or deviating. Many years of constant service, without disloyalty, also stirs up the power of God.

2. Stir it up by being aggressive and fast.

Whenever the angel of the Lord stirred up the waters, the person who jumped into the water first received his healing. This man was unable to do much for himself because everyone around him was faster and smarter at getting into the water.

Today, the kingdom of God is made up of those who press hard into it. You must apply pressure to stir up the power of God in your life.

The law and the prophets were until John: since that time the kingdom of God is preached, and every man presseth into it.

Luke 16:16

Because the man by the Pool of Bethesda was unable to apply more pressure and speed to his goal of experiencing the power of God, others received it whilst he did not. It is important to be very active and aggressive about experiencing God's power. The power of God is real.

However, there is very little you will see until you step out and act with speed, with faith and with aggression. If you do not act with speed, faith and aggression, your ministry will wait for "thirty-eight years" before it blossoms.

Notice that miracles were happening all around. It is not that there was no power available to heal the man sitting by this pool. The evidence of the power was in the fact that many people had been in the same situation but had gotten healed and gone home.

Dear friend, you are not the only person who has been called to be a pastor and an evangelist. You are not the only person God has called to be a missionary. You are not the only person with a bright future in God. I can assure you that there are many people who have as bright a future as you do. Perhaps, several young men just like you have been anointed and had hands laid on them. You are not the only person who has had a prophetic word spoken over your life. It is time to stir up the gift of God and experience His power practically by using speed, faith and aggression.

3. Stir it up by copying your father.

Each miracle of Jesus reveals a key to stirring up the gift of God. In the miracle of the Pool of Bethesda, you will see Jesus copying His Father.

Then answered Jesus and said unto them, Verily, verily, I say unto you, The Son can do nothing of himself, but

what he seeth the Father do: for what things soever he doeth, these also doeth the Son likewise.

John 5:19

Copying your father is a master key to stirring up the gift of God. Any time I have found myself copying a father that God has given to me, I have found myself going higher and experiencing the power of God. Every time you copy a father, you will find yourself partaking of the grace that is upon your father.

Even as it is meet for me to think this of you all, because I have you in my heart; inasmuch as both in my bonds, and in the defence and confirmation of the gospel, YE ALL ARE PARTAKERS OF MY GRACE.

Philippians 1:7

You must learn how to copy the preaching messages of your father. You must learn how to copy his style. You must learn how to copy his miracles. You must learn how to copy his strengths. Copying stirs up the power of God and releases you into a higher dimension. You can stir up the gift of God by copying the fathers God has given you.

4. Stir it up by compassion.

It is a blessing to see how the compassion and the love of Jesus also bring about miracles. The power of God was stirred up when Jesus walked up to the man under the instructions of the heavenly Father.

Then answered Jesus and said unto them, Verily, verily, I say unto you, The Son can do nothing of himself, but what he seeth the Father do: for what things soever he doeth, these also doeth the Son likewise.

John 5:19

The Father sees the suffering and the trouble that you are going through. The compassion of God will stir up the power

29

of God. This is why you see the phrase "Jesus was moved with compassion."

Jesus could have done all His great works without having any feelings of compassion. But He was filled with compassion, concern, kindness, sympathy and care for the suffering of people. God is a God of compassion, His ministers must also be full of compassion.

CHAPTER 6

Stir It Up, Nobleman

So Jesus came again into Cana of Galilee, where he made the water wine. AND THERE WAS A CERTAIN NOBLEMAN, WHOSE SON WAS SICK AT CAPERNAUM.

WHEN HE HEARD THAT JESUS WAS COME OUT OF JUDAEA INTO GALILEE, HE WENT UNTO HIM, AND BESOUGHT HIM THAT HE WOULD COME DOWN, AND HEAL HIS SON: FOR HE WAS AT THE POINT OF DEATH.

Then said Jesus unto him, Except ye see signs and wonders, ye will not believe.

The nobleman saith unto him, Sir, come down ere my child die.

Jesus saith unto him, Go thy way; thy son liveth. And the man believed the word that Jesus had spoken unto him, and he went his way.

And as he was now going down, his servants met him, and told him, saying, Thy son liveth.

Then enquired he of them the hour when he began to amend. And they said unto him, Yesterday at the seventh hour the fever left him.

So the father knew that it was at the same hour, in the which Jesus said unto him, Thy son liveth: and himself believed, and his whole house.

This is again the second miracle that Jesus did, when he was come out of Judaea into Galilee.

John 4:46-54

The nobleman's son's miracle is one of the four great healing miracles in the book of John.

The other three miracles are the healing of the man by the pool of Bethesda in the fifth chapter of John, the healing of the blind man in the ninth chapter of John and the raising of Lazarus in the eleventh chapter of John. Indeed, there are still many noblemen who need miracles from God. It is possible to stir up the miracle power of God for noblemen.

What exactly did the nobleman do to get himself in this amazing list of four miracles? The nobleman stirred up the power of God by doing three things. He heard of Jesus, he went to Jesus and he besought Jesus. These three things stirred up the power of God for the nobleman.

1. Stir it up by hearing.

When you hear the word of God, you are stirred up. There are times I have jumped up from my chair whilst listening to the word of God. Hearing the Word has always stirred me up. Sometimes, I am unable to stay in one place because I am greatly affected by what I am hearing. Faith comes by hearing!

As you hear the word of God, amazing changes take place in the spirit. He sent His Word and healed them.

> He sent his word, and healed them, and delivered them from their destructions.
>
> Psalm 107:20

The word of God that is coming towards you will surely stir up something supernatural in your life. In 1988, whilst listening to a message by Kenneth Hagin, my heart was stirred up and I received an anointing to teach.

On different occasions after that, I have found myself jumping and exclaiming to myself in amazement and in joy as I have listened to the Word.

33

One day, I was watching a video and listening to the word of God. When the man of God finished preaching, I blurted out to the man in the video, "*You are lovely!*" My spirit was so stirred up that it just came out of my spirit. Your spirit can be stirred up when you watch and listen to the word of God.

When the lights are out, your hearing increases and you begin to hear things you never heard before. Hearing the word of God will stir up the power of God in your life. The nobleman experienced a stirring when he heard of Jesus. That was the beginning of his miracle.

2. Stir it up by travelling.

The nobleman went to Jesus. There are many people who cannot lift their bodies out of their beds to even sit up to hear the word of God. Many people are too lazy to take a short journey hear the word of God. Jesus commended the Queen of Sheba because she travelled all the way to hear the wisdom of Solomon. By this, Jesus was commending all those who make special journeys to see and to hear the word of God.

Many years ago, I took a special journey to Tulsa, Oklahoma to see and hear Kenneth Hagin speaking. It was an important journey in my life. God blessed me through Kenneth Hagin.

For the last twenty years, I have been going regularly to Korea to sit under the ministry of David Yonggi Cho. My journey to Tulsa, Oklahoma stirred up the gift of a prophet and a teacher. My journey to Korea stirred up the pastoral gift and the anointing for church growth.

It is important that you make special journeys that will stir up the gift of God. The nobleman stirred up the gift of God by going to Jesus when He heard that he was in the Galilee area. Capernaum is a long way from Cana. The nobleman went all the way from Cana to Capernaum to see Jesus and ask for His help.

Travelling and moving will always stir up the power of God in your direction. There were many other noblemen and important people who probably had sick children. But none of them received a miracle, except the nobleman who travelled to see Jesus.

3. Stir it up by beseeching.

When the nobleman saw Jesus, he besought Him to come along to his house. This means that he pleaded and begged Jesus to come. The way you ask and plead reveals your faith, your love and your belief in the person's compassion.

When you express faith in someone's kindness and mercy, it stirs him up to be more merciful. Your hopeful eyes and your pleading eyes stir him up to be merciful. All he wants to do is to extend mercy because he sees that you expect mercy. You must come before God with hopeful and pleading eyes. God is full of compassion for you.

CHAPTER 7

Stir Up Abundance

And it came to pass, that, as the people pressed upon him to hear the word of God, he stood by the lake of Gennesaret, And saw two ships standing by the lake: but the fishermen were gone out of them, and were washing their nets.

AND HE ENTERED INTO ONE OF THE SHIPS, WHICH WAS SIMON'S, AND PRAYED HIM THAT HE WOULD THRUST OUT A LITTLE FROM THE LAND. AND HE SAT DOWN, AND TAUGHT THE PEOPLE OUT OF THE SHIP.

Now when he had left speaking, he said unto Simon, Launch out into the deep, and let down your nets for a draught. And Simon answering said unto him, Master, we have toiled all the night, and have taken nothing: NEVERTHELESS AT THY WORD I WILL LET DOWN THE NET. AND WHEN THEY HAD THIS DONE, THEY INCLOSED A GREAT MULTITUDE OF FISHES: AND THEIR NET BRAKE.

AND THEY BECKONED UNTO THEIR PARTNERS, WHICH WERE IN THE OTHER

SHIP, THAT THEY SHOULD COME AND HELP THEM. AND THEY CAME, AND FILLED BOTH THE SHIPS, SO THAT THEY BEGAN TO SINK. When Simon Peter saw it, he fell down at Jesus' knees, saying, Depart from me; for I am a sinful man, O Lord.

For he was astonished, and all that were with him, at the draught of the fishes which they had taken: And so was also James, and John, the sons of Zebedee, which were partners with Simon. And Jesus said unto Simon, Fear not; from henceforth thou shalt catch men. And when they had brought their ships to land, they forsook all, and followed him.

Luke 5:1-11

1. Stir it up by giving.

As Jesus came by the lake of Gennesaret, He was full of power to perform miracles. The miracle power of provision, of wealth, of supply and of abundance was walking on the beach. Who would stir up this miracle power? Who would stir up the gift of God?

It was Simon Peter who stirred up the gift of God by giving out his ship to the pastor. The ship, which was normally used for fishing, was now being used for preaching. Simon, who had nothing to do with the ministry, stirred up the gift of God by allowing himself and what he had to be used by God.

You can stir up the gift of God by giving and sowing seeds into the kingdom of God. Many years ago, we were having a fund-raising event to build our first cathedral. There were many rich people who gave bits and pieces here and there to support the work. Out of the blue, an unmarried lady who was a government worker stepped forward and donated a huge amount, which was probably everything she had, and even beyond what she had.

I suddenly felt a surge of compassion towards this unmarried lady and I felt the power of God moving over her life. No one had ever proposed to marry this lady. In the next few months, the miracle power of God flowed and God provided a husband for her. Mind you, it takes the power of God to get married.

There are millions of unmarried women in every country. Many women are used as sexual objects but not chosen as wives. It is a blessing and a miracle to be chosen to be someone's wife. That miracle happened to this lady shortly after she gave that amazing offering. It was not the amount, because she was not a rich person, but the gesture of giving more than she had to the Lord. That made all the difference!

When Peter gave his ship to be used for preaching, Jesus was greatly moved. The heavens were stirred. The power of riches and wealth was stirred up. The power of abundance was released. Peter's boat began to sink. Peter's life was changed. He had enough fish to last for months. He was the richest fisherman in the whole of Galilee.

Jesus was demonstrating the power of abundance in this remarkable story. We learn the keys to stirring up the power of abundance. You can stir up the power of abundance by giving

2. Stir it up by respecting the prophet.

Peter respected Jesus Christ. Peter respected Jesus, even though he did not know who He was. Obviously, he knew that He was a preacher. And that was all! Peter did not react wrongly to preaching and teaching. He had great respect for the ministry.

However, there could have been other possible reactions to Jesus' request. Peter could have said that, "My boat is not available for aimless wanderers who are strolling on the beach whilst we are working hard for a living." Peter could have said, "My boat was made for fishing and not for church activities." Peter could have said, "Purposeless men should not discourage those who are doing honest work."

Peter could have said, "Shall I leave the mending of my nets to push this unemployed carpenter-turned-preacher out into the water? Does he know the energy that is required to push boats into the water? Does he not know that the boat could drift away?"

Yet Peter did not say any of these things. He pleasantly and gladly gave up his ship for Jesus' use. That is how the power of miracle, finances and provision was released in the life of Peter.

3. Stir it up by respecting the Word.

It is important to respect the Word. Peter showed great respect for the word of God.

He said, "..., Master, we have toiled all the night, and have taken nothing: nevertheless at thy word I will let down the net" (Luke 5:5).

"At thy word…!" "At thy word…!" "At thy word…!"

It is important to respect the Word. When the word of God takes the highest position in your life, you are stirring up the power of God. As soon as Peter said, "At thy word," he was telling Jesus that he had great respect for His words. Peter was telling Jesus that His Words were more important than Peter's opinions.

Telling someone that his words mean so much is to express great love and trust in the person. Any time someone has told me that they would do what I say just because I am saying it, I have felt great power and compassion towards the person. I have a sensing of trying to do something to help the person, just because the person thinks that my words are important.

Every time God sees your response to His Word, He is seeing your response to Him as a Person. Remember that we are all in trouble because Adam and Eve set aside God's Word and trusted the serpent's word more. The Lord God was greatly offended that they would trust the serpent that they had just met, instead of He who created them and had given them such opportunities in the Garden of Eden.

Do not set aside the word of God and you will experience the power of God. Every word of God about every aspect of your life is important for you. At His Word, your life must change. At the word of God you must take important decisions. This will stir up the power of God in your life and ministry.

CHAPTER 8

Stir Up Super Miracles

When Jesus then lifted up his eyes, and saw a great company come unto him, he saith unto Philip, Whence shall we buy bread, that these may eat? And this he said to prove him: for he himself knew what he would do. Philip answered him, Two hundred pennyworth of bread is not sufficient for them, that every one of them may take a little.

One of his disciples, Andrew, Simon Peter's brother, saith unto him, There is a lad here, which hath five barley loaves, and two small fishes: but what are they among so many?

And Jesus said, MAKE THE MEN SIT DOWN. Now there was much grass in the place. So the men sat down, in number about five thousand. And Jesus took the loaves; and WHEN HE HAD GIVEN THANKS, he distributed to the disciples, and the disciples to them that were set down; and likewise of the fishes as much as they would.

When they were filled, he said unto his disciples, Gather up the fragments that remain, that nothing be lost. Therefore they gathered them together, and filled twelve baskets with the fragments of the five barley loaves, which remained over and above unto them that had eaten.

Then those men, when they had seen the miracle that Jesus did, said, This is of a truth that prophet that should come into the world. When Jesus therefore perceived that they would come and TAKE HIM BY FORCE, TO MAKE HIM A KING, he departed again into a mountain himself alone.

John 6:5-15

This is one of the greatest miracles of Jesus. Indeed, the multiplying of bread and fish is such an outstanding miracle that the people wanted to make Jesus a king after He performed this miracle. There is no other miracle where they wanted to make Jesus a king for doing the miracle. What stirred up such power of God?

1. Stir it up by calming down.

Jesus stirred up the greatest miracle with the greatest power by asking the people to calm down and sit down. The agitated crowd was forced to sit down, instead of standing up. There are many things God cannot do because you are standing up, agitated, worried and fretting. Today, the word of God to you is clear.

Be careful for nothing; but in every thing by prayer and supplication with thanksgiving let your requests be made known unto God.

Philippians 4:6

A flustered person who is running around from one emergency to another will not think clearly and will not hear from God. When you wait on God, you need to also make time to calm down until you can receive from the Holy Spirit. Sometimes it takes a number of days to calm down.

I have learnt to give myself time to calm down in the presence of God. Sometimes it will take several days before you are calm enough to hear from God. When the Levites were being separated unto their ministry, they were to stay in the tabernacle for at least seven days. Most ministers cannot be separate and alone with God for seven days. Why seven days? You need seven days because you also need time to calm down in His presence.

AND YE SHALL NOT GO OUT OF THE DOOR OF THE TABERNACLE OF THE CONGREGATION IN SEVEN DAYS, UNTIL THE DAYS OF YOUR CONSECRATION BE AT AN END: for seven days shall he consecrate you...

43

Therefore shall ye abide at the door of the tabernacle of the congregation day and night seven days, and keep the charge of the LORD, that ye die not: for so I am commanded.

Leviticus 8:33, 35

2. Stir it up by creating order.

He saith unto them, How many loaves have ye? Go and see. And when they knew, they say, Five, and two fishes. AND HE COMMANDED THEM TO MAKE ALL SIT DOWN BY COMPANIES upon the green grass. And they sat down in ranks, by hundreds, and by fifties.

Mark 6:38-40

Jesus caused the people to sit down in fifties and hundreds. Jesus created order out of the confusion. It was only after He had calmly driven away confusion that He was able to perform the great miracle. God is not the Creator of confusion. Wherever there is confusion, it does not come from God or the Holy Spirit. If it does not come from God it comes from the devil.

For GOD IS NOT THE AUTHOR OF CONFUSION, but of peace, as in all churches of the saints.

1 Corinthians 14:33

Demons are the agents of confusion. Wherever there is disorder, confusion, shabbiness and filth, there is always demonic activity. By simply clearing away the confusion, the deterioration, the dirt, the ruins and the entropy in the surroundings, demons were inhibited. Bringing order and arranging everybody in ranks of fifties and hundreds created an environment in which the Holy Spirit could operate.

As you travel around the world, you will come to recognize the kind of evil spirits that inhabit different areas. Different principalities and powers control different regions of the world. Different princes, principalities, dominions and thrones dominate their territories and cause certain things to prevail there. Satan is described as the one who turned this world into a wilderness.

Yet thou shalt be brought down to hell, to the sides of the pit. They that see thee shall narrowly look upon thee, and consider thee, saying, IS THIS THE MAN THAT MADE THE EARTH TO TREMBLE, THAT DID SHAKE KINGDOMS; THAT MADE THE WORLD AS A WILDERNESS, and destroyed the cities thereof; that opened not the house of his prisoners?

Isaiah 14:15-17

It is important to fight the picture of confusion and disorganisation in your environment. Disorder, confusion and disorganisation are the atmosphere for demonic activity. Confusion, disorder and disorganisation are evil works. Confusion is considered as one of the evil works in the world.

For where envying and strife is, there is CONFUSION AND EVERY EVIL WORK.

James 3:16

Fight to gain control of the confusion that is surrounding your ministry. If it is not clear who the leader is, fight to make things clear. If it is not clear who will succeed you, then there is confusion in your ministry. If you live in a mess, surrounded by confusion, filth and chaos, there is a lot of demonic activity around you.

Stir up the power of God by getting rid of the disorganisation, the half-finished projects, the dirty surroundings and the filthy environment that you operate in!

3. Stir it up by giving thanks.

Jesus stirred up the power of God by giving thanks. He did not even ask God for help. He did not ask God for miracles. He did not ask God for bread. He did not ask God for fish. He thanked God! His disciples and the men standing around watched to see what Jesus would say when he prayed; but He only thanked God.

So powerful is the prayer of thanksgiving that the place where the five loaves and two fish were multiplied is remembered as the place where Jesus gave thanks.

> The day following, when the people which stood on the other side of the sea saw that there was none other boat there, save that one whereinto his disciples were entered, and that Jesus went not with his disciples into the boat, but that his disciples were gone away alone; (Howbeit there came other boats from Tiberias nigh unto THE PLACE WHERE THEY DID EAT BREAD, AFTER THAT THE LORD HAD GIVEN THANKS:) When the people therefore saw that Jesus was not there, neither his disciples, they also took shipping, and came to Capernaum, seeking for Jesus.

John 6:22-24

Giving thanks stirs up the power of God and the gift of God. Giving thanks is an amazing spiritual act. Giving thanks releases power for more. When you show gratitude to someone, it releases the power for the person to do even more for you.

Sometimes, saying thank you can make the giver feel bad. Your effusive thanksgiving for such a small thing provokes the person to want to do more so that the thanksgiving would be commensurate with the gift given. Thanksgiving can be quite provocative. It can provoke the Father to pour out many more blessings.

Never forget that at the grave of Lazarus who had been dead for four days, Jesus simply said thanks again, and another mighty miracle erupted!

> Then they took away the stone from the place where the dead was laid. And Jesus lifted up his eyes, and said, FATHER, I THANK THEE THAT THOU HAST HEARD ME. And I knew that thou hearest me always: but because of the people which stand by I said it, that they may believe that thou hast sent me. And when he thus had spoken, he cried with a loud voice, Lazarus, come forth. And

he that was dead came forth, bound hand and foot with graveclothes: and his face was bound about with a napkin. Jesus saith unto them, Loose him, and let him go.

John 11:41-44

It is time for you to stir up the power of God by being thankful. Say thank you often! Praise God often! Be filled with the Holy Spirit by saying thank you and praising God. If you do not say thank you, you will start complaining. As you say thank you, the power of God will flow in your life.

CHAPTER 9

Stir Up Healing Power

And a certain woman, which had an issue of blood twelve years, And had suffered many things of many physicians, and had spent all that she had, and was nothing bettered, but rather grew worse, When she had heard of Jesus, came in the press behind, and TOUCHED HIS GARMENT. For she said, if I may touch but his clothes, I shall be whole.

And straightway the fountain of her blood was dried up; and she felt in her body that she was healed of that plague. And Jesus, immediately knowing in himself that virtue had gone out of him, turned him about in the press, and said, Who touched my clothes? And his disciples said unto him, THOU SEEST THE MULTITUDE THRONGING THEE, AND SAYEST THOU, WHO TOUCHED ME?

And he looked round about to see her that had done this thing. But the woman fearing and trembling, knowing what was done in her, came and fell down before him, and told him all the truth. And he said unto her, Daughter, thy faith hath made thee whole; go in peace, and be whole of thy plague.

Mark 5:25-34

1. Stir it up by hearing.

Faith is an unstoppable force through which you overcome difficulties and problems of your life. Through faith, the greatest mountain can be removed from your life. The woman with the issue of blood heard about Jesus Christ. Faith comes by hearing. Her faith greatly increased when she heard about Jesus.

The power of God was in Jesus Christ as He walked through the crowd. He was filled with the power that created the universe. He was walking in the midst of many sick people. Many people had problems that needed solutions.

Many people needed help but they did not stir up the gift of God in Jesus because they did not have the keys that the woman with the issue of blood had. The woman with the issue of blood had the key of faith that comes by hearing.

Faith is a mighty force, an unstoppable force that is used to subdue kingdoms, shut the mouth of lions and to quench violence of fire. When this woman tried the unstoppable power of faith which comes by hearing, she stirred the power of God. She had heard of Jesus and she saw Jesus as a source of power and a source of help. When she was a few metres away from Jesus, she said to herself, "If I touch the hem of His garments I shall be made whole."

Faith has two components: what you believe in your heart and what you say with your mouth. With the heart man believeth and with the mouth confession is made unto salvation (Romans10:10).

This woman of faith had heard about Jesus and believed in Him. Then she made a confession with her mouth that brought her healing. She said, "If I touch the hem of His garment I shall be made whole "(Mark 5:28).

Today, stir up the power of God and the gift of God by exercising faith.

49

2. Stir it up by contact.

Touching, physical contact or the laying on of hands is a basic and foundational principle in the kingdom of God. Through physical contact, miracle power is transmitted from one person to another.   When you touch someone with faith, power is transmitted. If you have faith, you can transfer the power of God by touching a person.

You must develop your faith in this great principle: the principle of laying on of hands and making physical contact. Do not be fixated with the traditional way of laying on of hands where hands are laid on your head. Laying on of hands on your head is just one version of that principle of contact, leading you to the transmission of power.

I remember hearing of a man of God who arrived at the airport and as he shook hands with the people who welcomed him, they fell down. I have experienced that before, where the people who were greeting me by shaking hands fell down. A handshake can lead to the transmission of power. A hug can also lead to the transmission of power.

When a dead man fell into the grave of Elisha and made contact with the bones of Elisha, he was revived. The lingering anointing that was in the bones of Elisha got into contact with the dead man and he came back to life! (2 Kings 13:20-21). Do you think that it was Elisha's hand that was laid on the dead man? Certainly not! It was the bones of Elisha that the dead man got into contact with!

It is important that you stir up the power of God by believing in physical contact. Kenneth Hagin never laid hands on my head but he did give me a warm handshake. I really cherish the handshake because it was the only physical contact, I had with him. I believe the power of God was transmitted through that handshake.

On another occasion, a man of God whom I wanted to pray for me, mystically grasped my hand for about five minutes. I could not believe what was happening. The power of God was transmitted into my hands and I became anointed to build a mega church. Even though this same man of God laid hands on my head later, I perceived that it was the handshake that was a source of transmission of God's power into my life rather than the laying on of hands on my forehead.

CHAPTER 10

Stir Up Miracles

Now when he had ended all his sayings in the audience of the people, he entered into Capernaum. And a certain centurion's servant, who was dear unto him, was sick, and ready to die. And when he heard of Jesus, he sent unto him the elders of the Jews, beseeching him that he would come and heal his servant.

And when they came to Jesus, they besought him instantly, saying, THAT HE WAS WORTHY FOR WHOM HE SHOULD DO THIS: FOR HE LOVETH OUR NATION, AND HE HATH BUILT US A SYNAGOGUE. Then Jesus went with them. And when he was now not far from the house, the centurion sent friends to him, saying unto him, Lord, trouble not thyself: for I am not worthy that thou shouldest enter under my roof: Wherefore neither thought I myself worthy to come unto thee: but SAY IN A WORD, and my servant shall be healed. For I also am a man set under authority, having under me soldiers, and I say unto one, Go, and he goeth; and to another, Come, and he cometh; and to my servant, Do this, and he doeth it.

WHEN JESUS HEARD THESE THINGS, HE MARVELLED AT HIM, AND TURNED HIM ABOUT, AND SAID UNTO THE PEOPLE THAT FOLLOWED HIM, I SAY UNTO YOU, I HAVE NOT FOUND SO GREAT FAITH, NO, NOT IN ISRAEL. And they that were sent, returning to the house, found the servant whole that had been sick.

Luke 7: 1-10

1. Stir it up by loving Israel.

The centurion in this story brought his dear servant to the attention of Jesus. Obviously, the centurion was a good person who loved his servants so much that he would seek healing for them. The centurion, although he was a Roman army officer, loved Israel. His love for Israel was no secret. Everyone around testified to his love for Israel. Loving Israel is a spiritual act. Loving Israel will stir up supernatural blessings in your life. There are a number of reasons why loving Israel as a nation will lead to the stirring up of the power of God.

a. Isaac blessed Jacob his son. Jacob, who became Israel, is blessed through the blessing that he received from his father.

b. Israel is blessed because the blessing of Abraham continues on to his grandson, Jacob. Abraham became a blessing to the whole world through Jacob.

   And I will make of thee a great nation, and I will bless thee, and make thy name great; and thou shalt be a blessing:

                                                              Genesis 12:2

c. Jacob's father, Isaac, cursed everyone who curses Jacob. There is therefore a curse on all those who fight against Jacob.

d. The psalmist proclaimed a blessing for all those who love Jerusalem and Israel.

   Pray for the peace of Jerusalem: they shall prosper that love thee.

                                                              Psalm 122:6

Based on all these scriptures, loving Israel opens you up to ancient supernatural words and blessings. The centurion opened himself up to great blessings when he loved Israel. His posting as an army officer to the barracks in Israel turned out to be a blessing for him because he fell in love with the nation, Israel.

You can stir up the power of God by loving Israel.

2. Stir it up by building churches.

The centurion also stirred up the power of God by building a synagogue for the Jews. Building a church stirs up the power of God. All through the Bible, you will find great blessings for those who build the house of God.

a. David evoked blessings from God when he even thought of building a church. God said to him, "You did well to even have such an idea."

And the Lord said unto David my father, Whereas it was in thine heart to build an house unto my name, thou didst well that it was in thine heart.

1 Kings 8:18

b. Solomon built the house of God and attracted the glory of God. Since the days of Moses, when visible glory was seen, it was only in the time of Solomon that the glory visibly appeared again.

Thus all the work that Solomon made for the house of the Lord was finished: and Solomon brought in all the things that David his father had dedicated; and the silver, and the gold, and all the instruments, put he among the treasures of the house of God ...

It came even to pass, as the trumpeters and singers were as one, to make one sound to be heard in praising and thanking the Lord; and when they lifted up their voice with the trumpets and cymbals and instruments of musick, and praised the Lord, saying, For he is good; for his mercy endureth for ever: THAT THEN THE HOUSE WAS FILLED WITH A CLOUD, EVEN THE HOUSE OF THE LORD; SO THAT THE PRIESTS COULD NOT STAND TO MINISTER by reason of the cloud: for the glory of the LORD had filled the house of God.

2 Chronicles 5:1, 13-14

c. Great favour is proclaimed on all those who decide to build the house of God. The favour of God is invoked when you turn towards the building of the church. God favours you when you favour the stones of the church. (Psalm 102:13-14).

Thou shalt arise, and have mercy upon Zion: For THE TIME TO FAVOUR HER, yea, the set time, is come. For thy SERVANTS TAKE PLEASURE IN HER STONES, and favour the dust thereof.

Psalm 102:13-14

3. Stir it up by humility.

The centurion stirred up the power of God by walking in great humility. He said that he was not worthy for Jesus to come into his house. That statement was a statement of humility.

Your words reveal your pride or your humility. The centurion's humility was revealed by his words. Every act of humility is a spiritual step that attracts the power of God. Why is this? God gives grace to the humble.

God gives power to the humble. In other words, grace is the power of God. Power was given to this humble centurion when he declared that he was not worthy for Jesus to come into his house.

You will stir up the power of God and attract grace when you walk in humility and lowliness.

But he giveth more grace. Wherefore he saith, God resisteth the proud, but giveth grace unto the humble.

James 4:6

4. Stir it up by great faith.

Perhaps the greatest step to stirring up the anointing in the centurion's miracle was when he asked Jesus to stand in one place and speak a word.

It is easier to believe that something powerful is happening when someone comes to your house.

It is easier to believe that the power of God is flowing into your life when hands are laid on you.

It is not that easy to believe that a miracle is happening when a word is spoken at a remote location. How does a word spoken in one place affect a situation far away?

Today, you can rise up and operate in great faith by believing in words that are spoken from distant places. Believe when a word is spoken that it is powerful and will come to pass. Great faith stirs up the anointing for miracles.

CHAPTER 11

Stir Up Signs and Wonders

And when Jesus was passed over again by ship unto the other side, much people gathered unto him: and he was nigh unto the sea. And, behold, there cometh one of the rulers of the synagogue, Jairus by name; and when he saw him, he fell at his feet, AND BESOUGHT HIM GREATLY, saying, My little daughter lieth at the point of death: I pray thee, come and lay thy hands on her, that she may be healed; and she shall live. And Jesus went with him; and much people followed him, and thronged him.

Mark 5:21-24

While he yet spake, there came from the ruler of the synagogue's house certain which said, Thy daughter is dead: why troublest thou the Master any further? As soon as Jesus heard the word that was spoken, he saith unto the ruler of the synagogue, Be not afraid, only believe. And he suffered no man to follow him, save Peter, and James, and John the brother of James. And he cometh to the house of the ruler of the synagogue, and seeth the tumult, and them that wept and wailed greatly.

And when he was come in, he saith unto them, why make ye this ado, and weep? the damsel is not dead, but sleepeth. And they laughed him to scorn. But when he had put them all out, he taketh the father and the mother of the damsel, and them that were with him, and entereth in where the damsel was lying. And he took the damsel by the hand, and said unto her, Talitha cumi; which is, being interpreted, Damsel, I say unto thee, arise. And straightway the damsel arose, and walked; for she was of the age of twelve years. And they were astonished with a great astonishment. And he charged them straitly that no man should know it; and commanded that something should be given her to eat.

Mark 5:35-43

1. Stir it up by humility.

The ruler of the synagogue found Jesus and fell at the feet of Jesus, beseeching Him. Please remember that these were rulers of the Jewish synagogue who arrested and crucified Jesus Christ. Jairus represented the wicked Jewish religious leaders who rejected Jesus Christ and cruelly put Him to death.

Jairus was a ruler of the synagogue, not a political or secular leader of society. It was odd to see such a strong figure of the religious society, falling at the feet of Jesus Christ.

Indeed, Jairus had been humbled by his daughter's illness and that is why he was so earnestly seeking the help of Jesus Christ. Humility is an important spiritual force. It activates blessings and draws the grace of God to your direction.

Pride does the opposite! Pride repels help. Pride repels God! Pride repels good people! Pride draws evil spirits to you. Pride opens you up to demonic activity. Proud people are usually easily offended, hurt, wounded and separated. Love (which is not arrogant) is not easily provoked. You will not be able to spiritually harm a humble person.

Walk in humility and you will draw great power to your direction. You will stir up the gift of God with humility. Whenever I encounter a humble person, I am drawn to the person. I always feel like helping humble people. I always feel like loving humble people. I feel zero attraction to proud and arrogant characters.

2. Stir it up by not being afraid to believe.

Jesus said to Jairus, "Fear not, only believe." Fear is negative faith. Jesus always comes with fear not, only believe! Today, you must reject fear and accept faith. There are many things to fear. There are many evils lurking around. Many bad things happen every day. There are many frightening stories that can make your heart stop.

It is a choice to believe that God will take care of you. It is a choice to believe that God will help you and cause you to see good days and good things. Without faith, you cannot carry on for a single day. Faith is important to stir up the gift of God. Fearing and thinking and worrying will only quench the Holy Spirit.

3. Stir it up by controlling the atmosphere.

Jesus stirred up the power of God by keeping the right company. He allowed only three disciples to follow Him. He did not invite Thomas and He did not invite Judas. Perhaps, it was such times where Judas was excluded that stirred him up to become treacherous. Jesus knew that He could not accomplish much for God in the presence of people who did not really believe in Him. It is important to control your atmosphere.

The atmosphere around you is basically controlled by the people who are around you. Human beings are the greatest atmosphere creators around you. An unhappy person creates a faithless environment.

A doubter and a sceptic create an environment which is difficult to operate in. I once had some pastors sitting on my stage when I was having miracle services. At a point I realised their presence was counter-productive to the miracle services. Just seeing them would quench my faith, and end the miracle service.

You can stir up the gift of God by ensuring that the people immediately around you are fully in the flow of all that you do.

4. Stir it up by casting out all your mockers.

I SAT NOT IN THE ASSEMBLY OF THE MOCKERS, nor rejoiced; I sat alone because of thy hand: for thou hast filled me with indignation.

Jeremiah 15:17

When Jesus got to Jairus' house, not only were people quietly doubtful but they openly mocked at Jesus. They mocked at Him and laughed at His proposal to raise Jairus' daughter from the dead. You must cast away all of your mockers. Their presence in your life is a provocation.

Are there not mockers with me? And doth not mine eye continue in their provocation?

Job 17:2

Indeed, the prophet Jeremiah refused to sit in the midst of mockers because he knew that their presence would quench the prophetic gift that was operating in his life.

5. Stir it up by making contact.

Jesus came to Jairus' house to perform a high-level miracle. He needed to stir up the power of God in a mighty way. He stretched out His hand and held Jairus' daughter, pulling her up. Jesus did not lay hands on her head to pray for her. He knew that any kind of contact would be a source of impartation to the young girl.

He physically made contact with her, fulfilling the principle of laying on of hands. Begin to stir up the gift of God by believing in physical contact. The physical contacts you make matter. Let every form of physical contact you make matter. Let it be of a spiritual quality that imparts and transmits the power of God.

God will use your handshakes, your hugs and all other forms of contact to minister His power.

6. Stir it up by speaking to the mountain.

Jesus performed this great miracle by speaking to the dead girl. Some of us do not even speak to the living. Jesus Christ went as far as communicating with the dead person.

He said to her, "*Talitha Cumi*" which is to say, "Young lady, I say to you, arise." Jesus had taught His disciples that they could speak to the mountain and command it to move if they had faith. In speaking to the dead body, Jesus was proving that His teaching on speaking to a mountain was real. There is nothing that is more of an unmoveable mountain than a dead body.

Beginning from today, you will speak to the dead, unmoveable issues in your life and they will start shifting! Stir up the gift of God by speaking to the mountains of your life!

CHAPTER 12

Stir Up Undeserved Miracles

And from thence he arose, and went into the borders of Tyre and Sidon, and entered into an house, and would have no man know it: but he could not be hid.

For a certain woman, whose young daughter had an unclean spirit, heard of him, and came and fell at his feet: THE WOMAN WAS A GREEK, A SYROPHENICIAN BY NATION; AND SHE BESOUGHT HIM that he would cast forth the devil out of her daughter.

BUT JESUS SAID UNTO HER, LET THE CHILDREN FIRST BE FILLED: FOR IT IS NOT MEET TO TAKE THE CHILDREN'S BREAD, AND TO CAST IT UNTO THE DOGS. AND SHE ANSWERED AND SAID UNTO HIM, YES, LORD: YET THE DOGS UNDER THE TABLE EAT OF THE CHILDREN'S CRUMBS.

And he said unto her, For this saying go thy way; the devil is gone out of thy daughter. And when she was come to her house, she found the devil gone out, and her daughter laid upon the bed.

Mark 7:24-30

1. Stir it up by seeking.

This lady, who was a Greek woman, came to seek Jesus. If you check your map you will discover that Greece is very far from Israel. Jesus Christ was nowhere near Greece and yet this Greek woman sought for Him in Israel.

We know that Jesus Christ did not travel any more than sixty-five miles from his birth-place. Jesus was close to home. But this woman from Greece, thousands of miles away, was seeking Him in Israel. The sense that someone is seeking you, desiring something from you, stirs up the gift of God. The sense that someone does not even notice your presence can quench your spirit. The opposite of that is to see someone who yearns for you, longs for you, desires your input and craves your touch.

Every seeker is a stirrer of the anointing. Whatever you have within you will be released when you encounter seekers. As soon as Jesus encountered this Syrophenician woman, the gift of God was stirred up in Him.

Ask and you shall receive, seek and you shall find!

2. Stir it up by unusual humility.

Stir up the gift of God by walking in unusual humility and not being offended.

The Syrophenician woman exhibited unusual humility. Unusual humility is exhibited when you are not offended and hurt by the things that satan uses to hurt you. Jesus said offences would surely come. No one can live in this world without being offended. The Syrophenecian woman was about to experience something that could offend her and send her to the deep end. I have watched pastors veer off into darkness when they were offended by something. An entire ministry destined for glory and eternal crowns can swerve away from the path of righteousness into deep darkness just because of hurts. Satan is the author of hurts, wounds and offences. Watch out for hurts, wounds and offences. They are the symptoms and signs of a satanic infiltration and penetration of your armour.

The Syrophenician woman stirred up the power of God by not being offended when she was compared with a dog. Jesus declared that He did not give bread to outside dogs. The fact that Jesus mentioned dogs in His illustration would offend many people. There are people who do not understand illustrations and immediately consider the mention of a dog in a sentence to be an insult.

Many people I know would have said that Jesus Christ insulted them and called them dogs. The Syrophenician woman was, however, not easily moved by Jesus' illustration. When you are not offended, you are exhibiting the highest kind of humility. Watch out for things that hurt you. You will drive away the power of God by your hurts, wounds and offences.

You will stir up the power of God by overcoming evil with good. Satan has thrown darts at you. Fiery darts are supposed to hurt you and make you wince and scream in pain. Satan loves to inflict hurts and injury to God's servants. He wants to wound you so much in your heart that you cannot rise up to minister in joy as you used to.

Your ability to lift up your head and to carry on in the service of God, even though you have been wounded, is a sign of your humility.

Priests were not allowed to have boils. A boil is an unhealed wound that is suppurating. These are wounds that go on and on, causing bitterness and spreading venom.

What kind of wounds do you have? Your wounds and hurts will only drive you away from the Lord's anointed. Your wounds and hurts are satan's efforts to cut you off from the gift of God.

Stir up the gift of God by walking in humility and not being offended.

CHAPTER 13

Stir It Up with Compassion

And it came to pass the day after, that he went into a city called Nain; and many of his disciples went with him, and much people. Now when he came nigh to the gate of the city, behold, there was a dead man carried out, the only son of his mother, and she was a widow: and much people of the city was with her. AND WHEN THE LORD SAW HER, HE HAD COMPASSION ON HER, AND SAID UNTO HER, WEEP NOT. AND HE CAME AND TOUCHED THE BIER: and they that bare him stood still. And he said, Young man, I say unto thee, Arise. And he that was dead sat up, and began to speak. And he delivered him to his mother. And there came a fear on all: and they glorified God, saying, That a great prophet is risen up among us; and, That God hath visited his people.

Luke 7:11-16

And Jesus went about all the cities and villages, teaching in their synagogues, and preaching the gospel of the kingdom, and healing every sickness and every disease among the people. But when he saw the multitudes, HE WAS MOVED WITH COMPASSION ON THEM, because they fainted, and were scattered abroad, as sheep having no shepherd.

Matthew 9:35-36

Jesus performed one of the greatest miracles ever heard of in the history of mankind. I do not know of any history book that records a man who raised another man from the dead at his funeral. There is no power like this power.

What is it that stirred up the gift of God so much in Jesus that He performed this great miracle at this funeral? Compassion in Jesus Christ was the key to this great miracle.

You do not experience great miracles in your ministry because you do not have compassion. Compassion is the master key to stirring up the miracle power of God. Pray that you will be filled with God's compassion. When compassion is flowing in your life, you will see the hand of God stirred up around you. Compassion makes all the difference. It is compassion that stirs up the gift of God. It is compassion that makes the difference in your ministry.

And of some have compassion, making a difference:

Jude 1:22

a. Notice that all the great miracles of Jesus were done through compassion. Great multitudes were healed because of the compassion of Jesus. Once Jesus had compassion, it was possible for miracles to happen.

But when he saw the multitudes, he was moved with compassion on them, because they fainted, and were scattered abroad, as sheep having no shepherd.

Matthew 9:36

b. God expects His servants to be filled with compassion. "Should you not have had compassion?" are the words of the Master. It is important for you to develop compassion in your heart. Hardness, wickedness and strictness are not helpful when you are trying to care for lost sheep. You will end up killing most of the sheep before they grow to their full age. Your impatience and severity will only kill off the weak ones. I can assure you, most of the people are weak.

God is expecting us to have His heart so that we can gently work with the weak people and show them His compassion.

Shouldest not thou also have had compassion on thy fellowservant, even as I had pity on thee?

Matthew 18:33

c. Compassion is a manifestation of the shepherd's anointing. Every anointed shepherd is filled with compassion for the sheep he is called to. Become an anointed shepherd today. Jesus has billions of followers because of His great compassion. He is the Good Shepherd. He is the great example for all pastors. He is full of compassion, full of mercy, full of love.

And Jesus, when he came out, saw much people, and was moved with compassion toward them, because they were as sheep not having a shepherd: and he began to teach them many things.

Mark 6:34

d. Compassion is a manifestation of God's powerful feelings. Our heavenly Father's feeling towards the lost human race is simply compassion and pity. We are completely lost and helplessly drowned in sin. We have very little ability to do what is right.

Our heavenly Father is always looking out of the window with pity and compassion. He watches us as we strive to come nearer to Him. All true shepherds must be filled with the same kind of compassion that the Father has towards His children. The elder brother who stayed at home had no such feelings of compassion for the lost child.

You must develop the Father's heart filled with compassion and you will soon be experiencing great miracles in your ministry.

And he arose, and came to his father. But when he was yet a great way off, his father saw him, and had compassion, and ran, and fell on his neck, and kissed him.

Luke 15:20

e. Pastors who do not have compassion cannot bring healing. A healing ministry is a result of compassion. If you just want to demonstrate power so that people will think you are a man of God, your ministry will never become what it is destined to be.

God is actually not happy with priests, Levites, pastors and ministers who do not have compassion. Without compassion you cannot work for God properly. Without compassion you cannot be used to pour in the oil and the wine.

You will notice that it was the Samaritan, who was not an official priest, who brought healing to the wounded traveller. He was not ordained, he was not consecrated but he had compassion. God used the man of compassion and bypassed the ordained, appointed and consecrated priests.

Dear ordained priest, you must stir up the gift of God by developing a heart of compassion. You must be moved by the things that move God! You must be hurt by the things that hurt God! You must feel sad about the things that make God feel sad!

And Jesus answering said, A certain man went down from Jerusalem to Jericho, and fell among thieves, which stripped him of his raiment, and wounded him, and departed, leaving him half dead. And by chance there came down a certain priest that way: and when he saw him, he passed by on the other side. And likewise a Levite, when he was at the place, came and looked on him, and passed by on the other side. BUT A CERTAIN SAMARITAN,

AS HE JOURNEYED, CAME WHERE HE WAS: AND
WHEN HE SAW HIM, HE HAD COMPASSION ON
HIM,

Luke 10:30-33

f. Compassion is a sign of the mature love of God. Love is
    always a sign of maturity. When you are mature, you will
    be filled with love. Love is a fruit of the Spirit. Fruits only
    appear when a tree is mature. Love only appears when you
    are a mature tree. Until you have compassion you do not
    have the love of God. The compassion you have is a sign
    of the maturity that you have attained in the ministry.

**But whoso hath this world's good, and seeth his brother
have need, and shutteth up his bowels of compassion
from him, how dwelleth the love of God in him?**

1 John 3:17

CHAPTER 14

Stir Up Great Things

And they came to Jericho: and as he went out of Jericho with his disciples and a great number of people, blind Bartimaeus, the son of Timaeus, sat by the highway side begging. And when he heard that it was Jesus of Nazareth, HE BEGAN TO CRY OUT, and say, Jesus, thou Son of David, have mercy on me.

AND MANY CHARGED HIM THAT HE SHOULD HOLD HIS PEACE: BUT HE CRIED THE MORE A GREAT DEAL, THOU SON OF DAVID, HAVE MERCY ON ME. And Jesus stood still, and commanded him to be called. And they call the blind man, saying unto him, Be of good comfort, rise; he calleth thee. And he, casting away his garment, rose, and came to Jesus. And Jesus answered and said unto him, What wilt thou that I should do unto thee? THE BLIND MAN SAID UNTO HIM, LORD, THAT I MIGHT RECEIVE MY SIGHT. AND JESUS SAID UNTO HIM, GO THY WAY; THY FAITH HATH MADE THEE WHOLE. And immediately he received his sight, and followed Jesus in the way.

Mark 10:46-52

1. Stir it up by crying out.

Blind Bartimaeus sat by the roadside on the way out of Jericho. It was his daily routine and all that he hoped for was a few pennies. Most beggars are harmless and he was ignored by most of the people who passed by. He could not see anyone but he could hear the sounds of the passers by. The day Jesus passed by was his best day. When he heard the sound of a crowd passing by he knew that something unusual was happening. When he heard that it was Jesus of Nazareth, he began to cry out.

In my distress I called upon the Lord, and cried unto my God: he heard my voice out of his temple, and my cry came before him, even into his ears.

Psalm 18:6

Every time you cry out, God hears you. It is good to speak to God. God listens to your prayers. God hears you the instant you speak. When Hezekiah cried to the Lord, the prophet did not even have a chance to walk through the courtyard before the response to Hezekiah's cry was heard. Blind Bartimaeus got the attention of Jesus. You can stir up the gift of God by getting the attention of Almighty God through your cries.

The righteous cry, and the Lord heareth, and delivereth them out of all their troubles.

Psalm 34:17

Keep crying to the Lord! He hears every cry and every shout!

2. Stir it up by refusing to be silenced.

Do not allow anybody to silence you. All through your ministry you will have people who will try to silence you and quieten you. Many of the people who hate your voice are offended and hurt. Some of the people who are trying to quieten you are idle. They do not have much to do.

I once saw a pastor who dedicated himself to criticizing a greatly respected man of God whom many people receive from. I almost fell off my seat when I saw his videos and postings. I could not believe my eyes as I watched this man rant and rave in anger against God's servant. As I watched, I received understanding.

This man had nothing to do. He once had a large church with many followers. His church was scattered and he was left with no one to preach to. In his idleness, all he could do was to attack various servants of God who were building churches and ministering to the body of Christ.

This man was filled with passion as he pointed out scriptures that contradicted the teachings of God's servants. If he were to have been given a needle and thread, he would have sewn up God's servant's mouth so that he would not speak again. Often, people want to silence you but you must refuse to be silenced.

Keep on preaching. Keep on praying. Keep on crying out in spite of those who want to silence you. Like blind Bartimaeus, you will activate the power of God through your persistence. Your persistence in serving God, in spite of your detractors and in spite of attempts to quieten you, will stir up the gift of God.

3. Stir it up by asking for mercy.

Asking for mercy stirs up the gift of God. Blind Bartimaeus could have demanded a miracle because he was a descendant of Abraham. He could have said, "Abraham's blessings are mine." He could have said, "I am a Jew. I am special. I am one of the sons of Jacob." Indeed, blind Bartimaeus had many rights but he did not mention any of these legal rights when he called on Jesus. He did not even say how long he had been sitting there. He just asked for mercy.

Many years ago, I encountered Kathryn Kuhlman's ministry. She was once asked what she believed about miracles. Why are some people healed and why are others left unhealed? She explained that she did not know why some are healed and why some are not healed. She just trusted in the mercy of God to touch people.

Initially, you may have reasons why healings must take place. You may have biblical reasons and numerous scriptures to back your claims, demands and requests. With time, you will lean more towards the mercy of God. You will trust in God's mercy more than anything else. Blind Bartimaeus was clever and he asked for the mercy of God. All he wanted was God's mercies to be applied to him.

Learn to ask for the mercy of God. By asking for mercy, you will activate the gift of God and stir up the anointing.

4. Stir it up by asking for big things.

When Jesus finally paid attention to blind Bartimaeus, He gave blind Bartimaeus an opportunity to speak. "What do you want?" He asked him. This was blind Bartimaeus' final test. After asking for mercy, blind Bartimaeus had the opportunity to ask God for what he wanted.

Would he ask for accommodation? Would he ask for a contribution? Would he ask for food? Would he ask for help with his rent? Would he ask for a job? Would he ask Jesus to speak a good word on his behalf? Would he ask for a wife?

Blind Bartimaeus was clever. He asked for his eyesight. He asked for what only God could do. Indeed, asking for big things that only God can do, stirs up the gift of God. Why is that? This is because asking for the great and literally impossible thing is a sign of your trust and your dependence on God.

Only God can do certain things.

CHAPTER 15

Stir It Up by Honour

Now a certain man was sick, named Lazarus, of Bethany, the town of Mary and her sister Martha. (IT WAS THAT MARY WHICH ANOINTED THE LORD WITH OINTMENT, AND WIPED HIS FEET WITH HER HAIR, WHOSE BROTHER LAZARUS WAS SICK.) Therefore his sisters sent unto him, saying, Lord, behold, he whom thou lovest is sick. When Jesus heard that, he said, This sickness is not unto death, but for the glory of God, that the Son of God might be glorified thereby. Now Jesus loved Martha, and her sister, and Lazarus.

John 11:1-5

Then said Jesus unto them plainly, Lazarus is dead....

Then when Jesus came, he found that he had lain in the grave four days already...

Jesus therefore again groaning in himself cometh to the grave. It was a cave, and a stone lay upon it. Jesus said, Take ye away the stone. Martha, the sister of him that was dead, saith unto him, Lord, by this time he stinketh: for he hath been dead four days. Jesus saith unto her, Said I not unto thee, that, if thou wouldest believe, thou shouldest see the glory of God? Then they took away the stone from the place where the dead was laid. And Jesus lifted up his eyes, and said, Father, I thank thee that thou hast heard me. And I knew that thou hearest me always: but because of the people which stand by I said it, that they may believe that thou hast sent me. And when he thus had spoken, he cried with a loud voice, Lazarus, come forth. And he that was dead came forth, bound hand and foot with graveclothes: and his face was bound about with a napkin. Jesus saith unto them, Loose him, and let him go.

John 11:14, 17, 38-44

Perhaps the miracle of the raising of Lazarus is the greatest of all miracles. To raise a man from the dead is unheard of. But to raise him from the dead after he has been buried for four days is an even more mind-boggling miracle. After four days in the grave, his body would be badly decomposed.

Indeed, a dead body's smell is noticeable after the first day, if you know what you are smelling. Most dead bodies begin to smell badly after three days. A bad odour begins two to three days after death in a process known as putrefaction. It is caused by bacteria in the intestines. These organisms do not die along with a person. Instead, after death, they begin eating through the intestines. After a few days, micro-organisms spread across the thighs and stomach. This actually produces a foul odour, similar to the scent of rotten eggs. After three days, the dead body will have a protruding tongue with fluid oozing from the mouth and nostrils.

Lazarus' body must have been terribly decomposed after four days. Remember that in those days there were no embalming chemicals. His sisters confirmed this reality. "Jesus said, Take ye away the stone. Martha, the sister of him that was dead, saith unto him, Lord, by this time he stinketh: for he hath been dead four days." (John 11:39)

The raising of Lazarus from the dead is the greatest miracle ever. Jesus performed the greatest miracle ever known to the history of mankind. This must have also been the greatest release of power in the human race. What stirred up the gift of God so powerfully?

Stir It Up by Honouring

Jesus did this miracle because He was honoured by the sisters of Lazarus. Honour stirs up the gift of God. Notice how the sisters of Lazarus honoured Jesus Christ. They honoured Jesus Christ by having Him in their home and giving Him comfort, food and rest from the public. Jesus really loved these two ladies.

They were special to Him. There are no other personalities in the New Testament who are described in this way.

Now Jesus loved Martha, and her sister, and Lazarus.

John 11:5

Jesus was honoured by Mary who wiped His feet with her hair. Even though Jesus would eat in their house, both Mary and Martha had not become familiar. They were not rude to Jesus and they did not speak about Him behind his back. They did not say bad and negative things about Jesus Christ.

Now a certain man was sick, named Lazarus, of Bethany, the town of Mary and her sister Martha. (It was that Mary which anointed the Lord with ointment, and wiped his feet with her hair, whose brother Lazarus was sick.)

John 11:1-2

Indeed, a prophet is not without honour except in his own country. Jesus was unable to do mighty works where He was not honoured. (Mark 6:4-5)

Even the Son of God who could raise the dead after four days was unable to perform miracles where He was not honoured. It is no wonder that the Holy Spirit is described as a dove. A dove is very sensitive to slight movements, jerky movements and any kind of threat from a human being. The anointing is equally very sensitive to respect, to appreciation and to honour. Where there is the slightest lack of respect and honour and appreciation, the anointing does not work.

Perhaps, the best example of this principle is found in the sixth chapter of Mark. At the beginning of this chapter, you see how Jesus was unable to perform miracles. The Son of God unable to heal people! Because of the lack of respect and appreciation, Jesus Christ moved away from those who dishonoured Him. He travelled away and went towards people who loved, respected and welcomed Him.

And he could there do no mighty work, save that he laid his hands upon a few sick folk, and healed them.

Mark 6:5

Throughout the sixth chapter of the book of Mark, we see amazing miracles taking place including the feeding of five thousand people. By the end of the sixth chapter of Mark sick people were being carried towards Jesus from all over the world, just so that Jesus would touch them and they would be healed. Jesus began the sixth chapter of Mark without honour and there were no miracles. He ended the sixth chapter of Mark as the miracle man whom the whole world sought after.

And ran through that whole region round about, and began to carry about in beds those that were sick, where they heard he was. And whithersoever he entered, into villages, or cities, or country, they laid the sick in the streets, and besought him that they might touch if it were but the border of his garment: and as many as touched him were made whole.

Mark 6:55-56

CHAPTER 16

Stir Up Manifestations

AND IT CAME TO PASS ABOUT AN EIGHT DAYS AFTER THESE SAYINGS, HE TOOK PETER AND JOHN AND JAMES, AND WENT UP INTO A MOUNTAIN TO PRAY. AND AS HE PRAYED, THE FASHION OF HIS COUNTENANCE WAS ALTERED, and his raiment was white and glistering. And, behold, there talked with him two men, which were Moses and Elias: Who appeared in glory, and spake of his decease which he should accomplish at Jerusalem. But Peter and they that were with him were heavy with sleep: and when they were awake, they saw his glory, and the two men that stood with him.

And it came to pass, as they departed from him, Peter said unto Jesus, Master, it is good for us to be here: and let us make three tabernacles; one for thee, and one for Moses, and one for Elias: not knowing what he said. While he thus spake, there came a cloud, and overshadowed them: and they feared as they entered into the cloud. And there came a voice out of the cloud, saying, this is my beloved Son: hear him. And when the voice was past, Jesus was found alone. And they kept it close, and told no man in those days any of those things which they had seen.

AND IT CAME TO PASS, THAT ON THE NEXT DAY, WHEN THEY WERE COME DOWN FROM THE HILL, MUCH PEOPLE MET HIM. And, behold, a man of the company cried out, saying, Master, I beseech thee, look upon my son: for he is mine only child. And, lo, a spirit taketh him, and he suddenly crieth out; and it teareth him that he foameth again, and bruising him hardly departeth from him. And I besought thy disciples to cast him out, and they could not. And Jesus answering said, O faithless and perverse generation, how long shall I be with you, and suffer you? Bring thy son hither. And as he was yet a coming, the devil threw him down, and tare him. And Jesus rebuked the unclean spirit, and healed the child, and delivered him again to his father.

Luke 9:28-42

1. Stir it up by waiting on God.

The gift of God is stirred up by waiting on God! The miracle of Jesus healing the young epileptic boy is a revelation on how to stir up the power of God. What did Jesus do to heal the boy? Why did the young boy go into convulsions when he saw Jesus? Why did he not have these manifestations with the disciples? The answer is simple. The disciples did not go up into any mountain to wait on God.

That is why Jesus went up into the mountain to wait on God. If you want to stir up the gift, you must go to mountains to wait on God. Those who do not go to the mountain to wait on God will never see such miracles in their ministry. Why do you call yourself a minister and not go to the mountains to wait on God? God is waiting for you to give Him some attention. When you give Him attention, you will reveal your love for Him. Waiting on God is the sign that you believe in God and that you love Him. The time spent on other things reveals the love you have for those things. The time you spend on your phone reveals your intense affection and love for frivolous, light-hearted chatter and social interaction. The time you spend waiting on God reveals how much time you have for your appointment with the Lord.

In the book of Leviticus, when priests were being appointed, they were to spend seven days in the tabernacle. They were not supposed to go out of the house of God until the seven days were up.

AND YE SHALL NOT GO OUT OF THE DOOR OF THE TABERNACLE OF THE CONGREGATION IN SEVEN DAYS, until the days of your consecration be at an end: for seven days shall he consecrate you.

Leviticus 8:33

It took seven whole days to consecrate and separate the priests for their work. Indeed, it is going to take at least seven days of waiting on God, praying, fasting and seeking God's face for you to stir up the gift of God.

It is important that you come away and wait on the Lord. They that wait on the Lord shall renew their strength (Isaiah 40:31). As you wait on God you become a stirred-up eagle who mounts up and flies. When you are not a stirred-up eagle, you become like a chicken who is fixed to the ground, who is unable to fly, unable to glide and unable to soar in the skies. Do you want to remain on the ground or do you want the gift of God to be stirred up in you?

2. Stir it up by prayer.

The gift of God in you is stirred up by prayer! What did Jesus go to do in the mountain? Was He making an omelette for Himself and having a feast with His disciples? Did Jesus go up into the mountain for a picnic? Indeed, He gave Himself to prayer. The Bible tells us clearly what Jesus did in the mountain.

> And it came to pass about an eight days after these sayings, he took Peter and John and James, and went up into a mountain to pray. And as he prayed, the fashion of his countenance was altered, and his raiment was white and glistering
>
> Luke 9:28-29

Prayer will activate the power of God. There is nothing that compares with prayer in a Christian's life. Prayer brings angelic interventions in your life. Prayer brings in the participation of angels. As soon as angels are involved in your life, you will begin to experience a supernatural turn of events. Supernatural things will be activated and stirred up because angels will be on the move.

Prayer changes things! Prayer changes you! Prayer makes you a different person. All your dormant spiritual gifts will be stirred up by hours of prayer.

3. Stir it up by faith.

Jesus explained why His disciples were unable to do the miracles. They were a "faithless and perverse generation". They had no faith!

And I besought thy disciples to cast him out; and they could not. And Jesus answering said, O FAITHLESS AND PERVERSE GENERATION, how long shall I be with you, and suffer you? Bring thy son hither. And as he was yet a coming, the devil threw him down, and tare him. And Jesus rebuked the unclean spirit, and healed the child, and delivered him again to his father.

Luke 9:40-42

Without faith you cannot do great things for God. Faith is partnering with the supernatural to accomplish the impossible. When you have faith, you have deployed a mighty force to help you to accomplish what ordinary people cannot accomplish. That is why men of faith can walk through the Red Sea! You cannot walk through the Red Sea unless you are using supernatural faith. Faith in God activates the supernatural. When you go away and wait on God, you will be filled with faith and the supernatural will be activated. Stir up the gift of God by walking by faith!

CHAPTER 17

Stir It Up Urgently

And as Jesus passed by, he saw a man which was blind from his birth. And his disciples asked him, saying, Master, who did sin, this man, or his parents, that he was born blind?

Jesus answered, Neither hath this man sinned, nor his parents: but that the works of God should be made manifest in him. I MUST WORK THE WORKS OF HIM THAT SENT ME, WHILE IT IS DAY: THE NIGHT COMETH, WHEN NO MAN CAN WORK. AS LONG AS I AM IN THE WORLD, I AM THE LIGHT OF THE WORLD.

When he had thus spoken, he spat on the ground, and made clay of the spittle, and he anointed the eyes of the blind man with the clay, And said unto him, Go, wash in the pool of Siloam, (which is by interpretation, Sent) He went his way therefore, and washed, and came seeing.

The neighbours therefore, and they which before had seen him that he was blind, said, Is not this he that sat and begged?

Some said, This is he: others said, He is like him: but he said, I am he. Therefore said they unto him, How were thine eyes opened? He answered and said, A man that is called Jesus made clay, and anointed mine eyes, and said unto me, Go to the pool of Siloam, and wash: and I went and washed, and I received sight.

John 9:1-11

1. Stir it up by urgency.

The Spirit of the Lord is upon me, because he hath anointed me to preach the gospel to the poor; he hath sent me to heal the brokenhearted, to preach deliverance to the captives, and recovering of sight to the blind, to set at liberty them that are bruised,

Luke 4:18

Jesus' mission was clear. He was anointed to recover the sight of the blind. Jesus Christ had a sense of urgency. I must work the works of Him that sent me while it is day. A man who is conscious of the time is a man of great works. He is always walking briskly, moving urgently and achieving the goals that have been set before him by the Lord.

Jesus was conscious of the approaching nightfall. He knew that He would not always have the opportunity that He had. Non-achievers do not stir up their gifts because there is no urgency.

When Jesus saw this blind man He knew that this was one of the few opportunities that He would have to give sight to the blind. He knew that He was anointed to give sight to the blind.

What has God anointed you for? What have you been sent to do? Do you realise that the night is coming? Do you realise that you are standing before one of the last opportunities to do certain things? When the night finally comes, you will wonder why you did not do many more of the things you were anointed to do. Were you anointed to build churches? Were you anointed to preach? Were you anointed to teach? Were you anointed to be a missionary? You will wonder why you did not do more of the things God has called you to do. A sense of urgency galvanises the gift of God into action. Develop a sense of urgency and you will find yourself accomplishing great things and stirring up the lion and the eagle that is in you.

2. Stir it up by using the anointing.

Jesus healed the blind man by the power of the Holy Spirit. He made an anointing substance with which He rubbed the man's eyes. Since He could not lay hands on any oil, He used His saliva with some nearby sand and rubbed the paste into the man's eye. What an amazing and practical Saviour we have! Somehow, He knew that He needed to have an anointing substance to minister to this man. Some people are not satisfied when a word is spoken over them. Some are not healed when hands are laid on them.

Some people want something more. This time Jesus did something more on the blind man. Stir up the gift of God by being practical and doing what will work for the moment. Improvise and administer the power of God in whatever way will work. The power of God will be activated when you step out in faith. The power of God will be activated when you step out using practical wisdom.

Since the man's eyes would be dirtied with the spittle and clay, Jesus asked the man to wash his face in the pool of Siloam. How hygienic and practical Jesus was in His ministry! Being hygienic and being practical do not in any way quench the Spirit.

You can stir up the gift of God by following the leading of the Holy Spirit: being practical and being wise.

CHAPTER 18

Stir It Up with Violence

And from the days of John the Baptist until now the kingdom of heaven suffereth violence, and the violent take it by force.

Matthew 11:12

And again he entered into Capernaum after some days; and it was noised that he was in the house. And straightway many were gathered together, insomuch that there was no room to receive them, no, not so much as about the door: and he preached the word unto them. AND THEY COME UNTO HIM, BRINGING ONE SICK OF THE PALSY, WHICH WAS BORNE OF FOUR. AND WHEN THEY COULD NOT COME NIGH UNTO HIM FOR THE PRESS, THEY UNCOVERED THE ROOF WHERE HE WAS: AND WHEN THEY HAD BROKEN IT UP, they let down the bed wherein the sick of the palsy lay. When Jesus saw their faith, he said unto the sick of the palsy, Son, thy sins be forgiven thee. But there were certain of the scribes sitting there, and reasoning in their hearts, why doth this man thus speak blasphemies? who can forgive sins but God only?

And immediately when Jesus perceived in his spirit that they so reasoned within themselves, he said unto them, why reason ye these things in your hearts? Whether is it easier to say to the sick of the palsy, Thy sins be forgiven thee; or to say, Arise, and take up thy bed, and walk?

But that ye may know that the Son of man hath power on earth to forgive sins, (he saith to the sick of the palsy,) I say unto thee, Arise, and take up thy bed, and go thy way into thine house. And immediately he arose, took up the bed, and went forth before them all; insomuch that they were all amazed, and glorified God, saying, We never saw it on this fashion.

Mark 2:1-12

Each of the miracles of Jesus teaches us a different lesson about stirring up the gift of God. In this story, we see four men who knew how to break into people's houses from the roof trying to help their friend to be healed.

The aggression, the persistence and the determination of these four gentlemen activated the power of God. They went to great lengths to see Jesus Christ. What lengths have you gone to, to see the Lord? How much physical effort do you put into your service to God?

The appearance of these people arriving through the roof stunned the onlookers. But Jesus was moved by their faith, their expectation and their belief in Him. The violence of these men was an expression of their faith. They did not speak a word to Jesus. They did not ask Him for anything. They only uncovered the roof and broke it. There are times your actions are much louder than your words. Your actions will say much more than any word you actually speak.

You may be called to the mission field. You may be called to preach the Word. You may be called to be an evangelist. You may also be wondering why the power of God is not flowing in your ministry.

When God called me to be an evangelist, there was no power flowing in my life and ministry. All I had experienced was a vision from God in which He told me to preach the gospel and pray for the sick. I did not have any miracles or a sign of miracles in my life. My actions would now prove whether I had faith or not! I organised myself a tent, a sound system and some lights and went out to find a field where I could preach the gospel. Without saying much and without inaugurating anything, my actions stirred up the power of God and miracles began to happen and people began to be saved.

Violent aggression and steps towards your calling will always stir up the gift of God in your life and ministry.

CHAPTER 19

Stir It Up and Release the Captives

And HE WAS TEACHING in one of the synagogues on the sabbath. And, behold, there was a woman which had a spirit of infirmity eighteen years, and was bowed together, and could in no wise lift up herself. AND WHEN JESUS SAW HER, HE CALLED HER TO HIM, AND SAID UNTO HER, WOMAN, THOU ART LOOSED FROM THINE INFIRMITY. AND HE LAID HIS HANDS ON HER: AND IMMEDIATELY SHE WAS MADE STRAIGHT, AND GLORIFIED GOD. And the ruler of the synagogue answered with indignation, because that Jesus had healed on the sabbath day, and said unto the people, There are six days in which men ought to work: in them therefore come and be healed, and not on the sabbath day. The Lord then answered him, and said, Thou hypocrite, doth not each one of you on the sabbath loose his ox or his ass from the stall, and lead him away to watering? AND OUGHT NOT THIS WOMAN, BEING A DAUGHTER OF ABRAHAM, WHOM SATAN HATH BOUND, LO, THESE EIGHTEEN

YEARS, BE LOOSED FROM THIS BOND ON THE SABBATH DAY? And when he had said these things, all his adversaries were ashamed: and all the people rejoiced for all the glorious things that were done by him.

Luke 13:10-17

1. Stir it up by teaching.

Stir up the gift of God through the teaching ministry. Teaching stirs up spiritual delights. The healing anointing is stirred up by teaching. When you teach the word of God, the faith of the congregation increases. Faith comes by hearing! The more you hear the word of God, the more your faith increases. Faith is a supernatural force. The supernatural power of God is therefore stirred up as you teach the word of God.

If you talk about something, your interest in that thing increases. Your desire for that thing increases. As you talk about miracles and the power of God, your desire for miracles and the power of God increases. The key to drawing out more of the power of God is to desire it. That is why the scripture teaches us to covet earnestly the best gifts. Teaching about something stirs up the desire for it. Teaching causes you to covet the power of God. As you covet the gift of God, you start to see the manifestations.

2. Stir it up by anger.

The gift of power in Jesus Christ was stirred up when He noticed the works of the devil. Jesus Christ was sent into this world to destroy the works of the devil. Everyone is stirred up by his enemy. You are energised and motivated when you sense the wickedness of your enemy. "Behold, all they that were incensed against thee shall be ashamed and confounded: they shall be as nothing; and they that strive with thee shall perish" (Isaiah 41:11). This scripture shows that your enemy can be incensed against you. When Jesus saw the extent of wickedness that had been done to the woman who was bowed over, He was furious. He wanted to drive out the devil.

You must notice works of the devil. They are works of your archenemy. You must see the wickedness, the anarchy, the confusion and the disloyalty that is generated by devils. You must be angry at the sicknesses, diseases and death caused by the devil.

Jesus was angry at what satan had done to this woman. He had made her bend over like a dog for eighteen long years. This alone stirred up the gift of God in Jesus to set her free.

Once I attended a funeral in England. The cemetery was vast and we had to drive a long way to find the grave. As we drove, I noticed endless rows of tombstones. The cemetery was so vast that it seemed to never end. I thought of all the dead people who were buried there. I thought of the tears that had been shed in this cemetery. I thought of the numerous final "goodbyes" that had been said to loved ones. I wondered how each one of these thousands of people had died.

Most of them must have been in hospital with various diseases. I thought of the numerous diseases and pathologies that must be buried under the earth in the cemetery. Who caused it? I thought of how satan had destroyed the world. I thought of how satan had inflicted such sorrow on the human race. Satan is a very wicked being.

Seeing what the devil has done to God's creation should cause anger to well up in you. Your anger at the devil and his deceptions should stir up the wrath of God in you. When you see cripples, the blind, the deaf and other forms of handicaps, you must be moved with compassion to undo the works of the devil.

One day, I found out my church member had a difficulty with sin. As I went into the case, I found out how she had been tricked, deceived, used and abused. When I saw how the devil had made mincemeat of the young lady, I was moved with compassion. My shepherding anointing was stirred up in me. I wanted to care for her, help her and lift her out of the mud she was in. You must be moved and angered when you see what satan has done.

If you just pass by unaffected when you see wicked things that satan has done, the gift of God will not be stirred up. From today, as you see the works of the devil everywhere, the gift of God will be stirred up in you. You will be anointed to reverse satanic works.

I was once in Cologne, a city in Germany. As I walked in the city centre, I saw thousands of people busy on the streets, walking, talking and chatting. I thought to myself, "How many of these people know about Jesus?" I was moved with compassion and the gift of evangelism was stirred up in me. I began to intercede for the souls of the thousands of lost Germans.

At another time, I was driving from Ghana to Mali to conduct a crusade. Late in the evening, we came across a solitary town made of huts and makeshift structures. This little town was in the north-western corner of Burkina Faso, at the border with Mali. I wondered when any church would ever be built in this corner and if the people in this area of the world would ever hear the gospel in their lifetime. The isolation and the threat of eternal damnation of these people began to stir up the gift of God in me. I wanted to have an evangelistic campaign there. I wanted to step out of the car and go witnessing. I wanted to reverse the works of the devil.

Noticing the desolation of people and how satan has earmarked people for hell stirred up the gift of God in me.

3. Stir it up by calling those things that are not as though they are.

God's power is stirred up when you call those things that are not as though they are.

Stir up the gift of God by calling those things that be not as though they are. God calls those things that are not as though they are. Jesus activated the power of God by speaking the word of faith to the woman. He said, "Woman, thou art loosed from thine infirmity" (Luke 13:12). In other words, it has already happened. You are set free!

Faith calls those things that are not as though they are. You must therefore call those things that are not as though they are. If you want to please God in your ministry, you must learn to minister to people by calling those things that are not as though they are.

Stand over problems, difficulties and wickedness of devils and call those things that are not as though they are. Stand over the ugliness inflicted by the devil and call it beautiful. Stand over the devastation wrought by demons and declare restoration. Stand over the barrenness, the emptiness and the wilderness which satan has produced and declare that it is a fruitful field. Stand over the parched, dry and desolate ministry and call it a place of abundance, growth and increase. You will stir up the gift of God by calling those things that are not as though they are. The power of God will be stirred up as you call those things that be not as though they were.

4. Stir it up by combining faith with the laying on of hands.

In this great miracle, Jesus combined two methods to stir up the gift of God. He "called those things that be not as though they were" and, in addition, He laid hands on the woman. Jesus stirred up the power of God by using these two spiritual keys.

Sometimes, you need to combine two things to stir up the power of God. Learn to combine keys that can stir up the gift of God.

CHAPTER 20

Stir It Up and Complete It

AND HE COMETH TO BETHSAIDA; AND THEY BRING A BLIND MAN UNTO HIM, AND BESOUGHT HIM TO TOUCH HIM. And he took the blind man by the hand, and led him out of the town; and when he had spit on his eyes, and put his hands upon him, he asked him if he saw ought. AND HE LOOKED UP, AND SAID, I SEE MEN AS TREES, WALKING. AFTER THAT HE PUT HIS HANDS AGAIN UPON HIS EYES, AND MADE HIM LOOK UP: and he was restored, and saw every man clearly. And he sent him away to his house, saying, Neither go into the town, nor tell it to any in the town.

Mark 8:22-26

1. Stir it up by touching.

The gift of God in Jesus was stirred up when the blind man asked that He touch him. How moving it must have been for Jesus to hear someone begging to be touched by Him!

It is important to cause people to have faith in the principle of laying on of hands. When people have faith in the laying on of hands, they have faith in physical contact. I remember seeing crowds of people thronging the crusade stage staircase. These were sick people who wanted to be touched and prayed for. They pressed forward to the stage and wrestled with each other to come onto the stage and receive a touch. There were times I wondered why these people would want me to touch them. The people had so much faith in receiving a touch from me This stirred me up. Desiring someone to touch you is moving. It moves the bowels of compassion. It stirs up the gift of God.

2. Stirred up by seeing incomplete works.

Incomplete works stir up the gift of God! The gift of God is stirred up to complete whatever has been started. When Jesus realised that the man saw men as trees walking, the anointing was stirred up again. The power of God flowed so that the man's eyesight could be perfect. What is the point in seeing men as trees? Then what will you see real trees as? Jesus' work of performing a miracle of healing was not complete. Jesus was stirred up to complete His miracle ministry.

Anything that is incomplete stirs up the anointing. Jesus wanted to stir up the evangelistic anointing by calling the disciples to look at the whitened fields of harvest. Looking at the fields of harvest will always stir up the ministry of the evangelist. Looking at the fields of harvest that were white and ready would stir up the soul winner's zeal.

> Say not ye, There are yet four months, and then cometh harvest? behold, I say unto you, Lift up your eyes, and look on the fields; for they are white already to harvest.
>
> John 4:35

It is important to finish what has been started. Any incomplete work of God stirs up the gift of God. When Nehemiah saw the broken walls of Jerusalem, he was stirred up to build them. The building anointing rose up in him to ensure that the walls of Jerusalem were completed.

Uncompleted church buildings, uncompleted ministries and uncompleted callings must stir you up to do even more for God. Whatever you have not finished must be finished. Allow the power of God to flow towards you so that you can finish what God has called you to do.

Look around you and see the unfinished job of your ministry. Your ministry is not finished. Has God done all that He said He would do? Have you gone as far as you are supposed to? Recently, as we prayed for the nations, I could see how incomplete my ministry was. I could see how shallow my ministry was. I was stirred up to build more churches, to send more missionaries and to do more crusades. I wanted to win more souls for Jesus. The apostolic, evangelistic and pastoral anointings were stirred up by seeing the uncompleted works before me.

Stir it up by looking at the uncompleted works all around you!

CHAPTER 21

Stir It Up Directly

And again, departing from the coasts of Tyre and Sidon, he came unto the sea of Galilee, through the midst of the coasts of Decapolis. And they bring unto him one that was deaf, and had an impediment in his speech; and they beseech him to put his hand upon him. And HE TOOK HIM ASIDE FROM THE MULTITUDE, AND PUT HIS FINGERS INTO HIS EARS, AND HE SPIT, AND TOUCHED HIS TONGUE; AND LOOKING UP TO HEAVEN, HE SIGHED, and saith unto him, Ephphatha, that is, Be opened. And straightway his ears were opened, and the string of his tongue was loosed, and he spake plain.

Mark 7:31-35

1. Stir it up by going aside from multitudes.

As you separate yourself from multitudes, you will stir up the power of God in your life.

Jesus stirred up the power of God by taking the deaf man aside from the multitude (Mark 7:33). Many of the greatest miracles that Jesus performed were done in private. Jesus often moved away from the masses and did great things in private. Large numbers of human beings and popular opinions do not often generate the holy presence of God. Human beings are generally evil and large numbers of human beings, multiply the evil attitudes and wicked sentiments.

When the crowds are gathered together, evil boils over. Popular opinions are often unspiritual opinions. Notice how Jesus sensed evil when the thick crowd gathered together. "And when the people were gathered thick together, he began to say, This is an evil generation: they seek a sign; and there shall no sign be given it, but the sign of Jonas the prophet" (Luke 11:29). There is much evil in the opinions and ideas of multitudes.

When Jesus was being tried by Pilate, it was a multitude which called for His murder.

"And there was one named Barabbas, which lay bound with them that had made insurrection with him, who had committed murder in the insurrection. And THE MULTITUDE crying aloud began to desire him to do as he had ever done unto them" (Mark 15:7-8).

Multitudes are dangerous groups. Indeed, never follow the mind and attitude of the multitude. Follow God and follow God's Word.

You will also notice how evil multiplied against Moses when the crowds gathered together. The popular thinking about Moses was evil and wrong. The crowd was wrong. The multitude was wrong. The vote against Moses was wrong. The popular opinion in the crowd was that Moses should be overthrown and replaced. "And all the congregation lifted up their voice, and cried; and the people wept that night. And all the children of Israel murmured against Moses and against Aaron: and the whole congregation said unto them, Would God that we had died in the land of Egypt! or would God we had died in this wilderness! And wherefore hath the LORD brought us unto this land, to fall by the sword, that our wives and our children should be a prey? were it not better for us to return into Egypt? And they said one to another, Let us make a captain, and let us return into Egypt" (Numbers 14:1-4).

2. Stir up by direct contact.

Jesus put His finger into the deaf man's ears and touched his tongue. He wanted to lay hands directly on that part of the man that was diseased. A person with difficulty in speaking is often a person with a difficulty in hearing. Jesus laid hands on the man's ears to bring healing to his hearing. Then He laid hands on the man's tongue to bring healing to his speech. Jesus did not want to just lay hands on the man's head. He wanted direct contact with the sick organs. Making direct contact with the man's ears and with his tongue stirred up the gift of God. It brought the power of God into play. Do not be afraid of direct contact. The power of God literally flows through contacting the body. The more you believe these things, the more you see the power of God activated in your life.

3. Stir it up by spitting.

Jesus spat and laid hands on the man's tongue. It is obvious that He transmitted His bodily fluids to the sick man. Today, many people would not accept this kind of ministration. In the light of the corona virus pandemic, it will not be easy to spit into other people's mouths. But that is what Jesus Christ did and the deaf and the dumb spoke. Jesus had better results in healing the dumb than we are having today with all our medical science. Indeed, spitting is taking the principle of laying on of hands to the extreme. It is causing the internal part of a body to come in contact with the external part of another body.

4. Stir it up by looking up to heaven.

The last thing that Jesus did was to look up into the sky. Looking up to God and trusting Him for a breakthrough is always the right thing to do.

CHAPTER 22

Stir It Up with Persistence

The law and the prophets were until John: since that time the kingdom of God is preached, and every man presseth into it.

Luke 16:16

And when Jesus came into the ruler's house, and saw the minstrels and the people making a noise, He said unto them, Give place: for the maid is not dead, but sleepeth. And they laughed him to scorn. But when the people were put forth, he went in, and took her by the hand, and the maid arose. And the fame hereof went abroad into all that land.

And when Jesus departed thence, TWO BLIND MEN FOLLOWED HIM, CRYING, AND SAYING, THOU SON OF DAVID, HAVE MERCY ON US. AND WHEN HE WAS COME INTO THE HOUSE, the blind men came to him: and Jesus saith unto them, Believe ye that I am able to do this? They said unto him, Yea, Lord. Then touched he their eyes, saying, According to your faith be it unto you. And their eyes were opened; and Jesus straitly charged them, saying, See that no man know it.

The miracle of the two blind men who followed Jesus all the way from Jairus' house until He entered another house, illustrates how persistence stirs up the gift of God. Jesus had had a hectic day. In one day, He had healed the woman with the issue of blood, the mad man of Gadara and Jairus' daughter. He was exhausted, as He tried to get home. However, two blind men were stubbornly determined to make contact with Jesus and make sure that He healed them too. How the two blind men were able to see where Jesus was going, I do not know.

Persistence led to the miracle of the two blind men being healed. They followed Jesus even into His house. When Jesus asked them what they wanted, they stubbornly repeated their request to have their sights restored to them. They were not going to take no for and answer and they were not prepared to stop following Jesus until they had what they wanted.

Persistence will stir up the gift of God. Years ago, I heard of David Yonggi Cho. I read about his amazing church where seven hundred thousand members would gather every Sunday. I wanted to make contact with this great man of God and somehow receive an impartation of the church growth anointing.

However, when I first tried to make contact with Yonggi Cho by trying to meet him in Switzerland, I was unable to. I kept trying to get closer to this great man of God. One day, after almost twenty years, I was having lunch with Yonggi Cho and opposite me was a man whom I had first met in Switzerland. He said to me, "You have done well. You have persisted." Indeed, I had persisted in trying to forge the right relationship with God's servant. I was undaunted by the setbacks and by the impediments that stood in my way. I believe that I have received a grace for church growth by associating with this great man of God.

The gift of God was stirred up by persistence. Through persistence, I have come to enjoy phenomenal church growth and increase. What gift do you desire? What manifestations do you seek? Persistence is one of the keys to stir up the gift of God.

CHAPTER 23

Stir It Up and Cast It Out

And they went into Capernaum; and straightway on the sabbath day he entered into the synagogue, and taught. And they were astonished at his doctrine: FOR HE TAUGHT THEM AS ONE THAT HAD AUTHORITY, AND NOT AS THE SCRIBES.

AND THERE WAS IN THEIR SYNAGOGUE A MAN WITH AN UNCLEAN SPIRIT; AND HE CRIED OUT,

SAYING, LET US ALONE; WHAT HAVE WE TO DO WITH THEE, THOU JESUS OF NAZARETH? ART THOU COME TO DESTROY US? I KNOW THEE WHO THOU ART, THE HOLY ONE OF GOD.

And Jesus rebuked him, saying, Hold thy peace, and come out of him.

And when the unclean spirit had torn him, and cried with a loud voice, he came out of him.

And they were all amazed, insomuch that they questioned among themselves, saying, What thing is this? what new doctrine is this? for with authority commandeth he even the unclean spirits, and they do obey him.

Mark 1:21-27

Stirring by Authority

Preaching with authority stirs up the gift of God. Jesus stirred up the devil in a man who was in the synagogue. This man was a regular church member and he fitted in perfectly with the society and with the congregation. No one saw him as having a problem. When Jesus visited the church, He preached with authority. The power of God was present.

Remember the word of God is the sword of the Spirit. Every time the preaching goes forth, a sword goes forth, cutting into the enemy and slicing into evil powers. That day in the synagogue, the sword of the Spirit went straight into the heart of the demons that had lived happily in this man for years. The man shouted, "Leave us alone. What have we to do with thee?" The reaction of the devils was a reaction to the word of God.

Preaching the word of God with authority will stir up the gift of God. When Jesus preaching was put side by side with the preaching of the Pharisees, the difference was clear. The Pharisees spoke with uncertainty, hesitancy and a lack of anointing. Jesus spoke with power, anointing and clarity. There is no need to copy messages and preach about things you do not fully understand. You must preach with authority. You must not preach hesitatingly and without authority. You must preach as inspired by the Holy Spirit.

Pastors who do not spend time in prayer and waiting on God are no different from school teachers or university lecturers. A university lecturer does not need the anointing or the power of the Holy Spirit. A university lecturer needs the facts and information. He does not need the anointing.

If you want to stir up the power of God, you need to be like Jesus. Jesus was an ordinary carpenter. Jesus' background was carpentry. Most likely, He was an apprentice to His earthly "father". Jesus was not there at the synagogue to present scientific research papers. He was speaking the heavenly words of God. He was speaking with authority. He was the living Word, speaking the words of God.

Stirring by Rebukes

Jesus released the power of God by giving a stunning rebuke to the devil. Many people need stunning and sharp rebukes. Jesus rebuked the devil sharply. People standing by in the synagogue would have thought, "Why is He speaking so sharply or rudely to this man?" Indeed, He was speaking to the devil and that devil needed a sharp rebuke to eject him from his habitation. Do you want to see the power of God? Learn to rebuke the devil sharply!

I once met a pastor who agreed with all sides. No matter who came to see him, he would flow along with the person's ideas. He was simply afraid to take a stance and look unpopular or unreasonable with any party. In the end, he lost the support and the love of both sides. Jesus was not like that. He was liked by some and hated by others. Every good leader will be liked by some and hated by others. Watch out for people who seem to be acceptable to all sides and all groups. There is nothing like that. You will either love one or hate the other. Most people who seem to flow with all sides, secretly support one side.

You can stir up the power of God by rebuking demons sharply. Rebuking demons will often look like you are rebuking a human being sharply. Do not draw back from your responsibility. Stir up the gift of God by walking in authority and rebuking the enemy sharply.

CHAPTER 24

Stir It Up by Personal Interaction

And forthwith, when they were come out of the synagogue, they entered into the house of Simon and Andrew, with James and John. But Simon's wife's mother lay sick of a fever, and anon they tell him of her. AND HE CAME AND TOOK HER BY THE HAND, AND LIFTED HER UP; AND IMMEDIATELY THE FEVER LEFT HER, and she ministered unto them.

Mark 1:29-31

S tir it up by personal contact. Jesus Christ ministered to Peter's mother-in-law. How did that happen? Jesus went to Peter's house. In this house, He was to receive personal attention, care and comfort. Jesus Christ was by now a personal friend to the house of Peter. This personal interaction stirred up the gift of God in Jesus Christ and a miracle happened for Peter's mother-in-law.

There are many miracles that happen only on direct interaction. The apostle Paul said, "I long to see you that I may impart some spiritual gift to you."

For I LONG TO SEE YOU, that I may impart unto you some spiritual gift, to the end ye may be established;

Romans 1:11

One day, I was talking to a prophet and he said to me, "When I see someone and interact with him, I often have a vision or dream about that person. At home or in my church, I may not have a vision, dream or revelation. But when I am close to them for a whole day, I may have a vision or revelation about them."

On another occasion I heard a prophet say that when he laid hands on people, he would have visions about them.

It looks like personal contact stirs up the gift of God.

Personal contact provokes visions and revelations to flow. Personal interaction can stir up the anointing of God. On the other hand, you must make sure that personal interaction does not stir up familiarity in you. Do not become proud because God's servant has come close to you.

Many stirrings of the gift of God happen when personal interaction happens. It is no wonder that the power of God that could heal fevers was manifested when Jesus came into direct personal interaction with Peter's home. Do not miss the opportunity for personal interaction with God's servant.

Giftings will be stirred up by personal interaction. Anointings will be stirred up because of the personal interaction you are experiencing. Expect great things to happen in your life and ministry if God opens the door for you to have a personal interaction with His servant.

CHAPTER 25

Stir It Up by Common Sense

And it came to pass, as he went into the house of one of the chief Pharisees to eat bread on the sabbath day, that they watched him. And, behold, there was a certain man before him which had the dropsy. And Jesus answering spake unto the lawyers and Pharisees, saying, Is it lawful to heal on the sabbath day? And they held their peace. And he took him, and healed him, and let him go; and answered them, saying, Which of you shall have an ass or an ox fallen into a pit, and will not straightway pull him out on the sabbath day? And they could not answer him again to these things.

Luke 14:1-6

Jesus would never have experienced this great miracle if He were not to put aside religious tradition. Jesus would not have experienced this great power if He had not followed common sense and simple logic. There are things you are missing out on because you are not using common sense. You are missing miracles, you are missing the will of God and you are missing the power of God because your aim is not simply to do well in the sight of God.

Stir it up by common sense! Sometimes we become so religiously brainwashed that the gift of God is not able to operate.

Jesus explained His logic in healing the man with the dropsy on the Sabbath day. He explained that an ass or an ox fallen into a pit would be pulled out on the Sabbath day. No one would consider that it was illegal to pull a donkey out of a pit on a Sabbath day. The donkey that was worth far less than human life was considered worthy of salvation, deliverance and healing on the Sabbath day. Why would a human being not be considered worthy of similar salvation, healing and deliverance?

Many people depart from God because they cannot face the truth about the things we believe. There are several logical, common sense reasons why you should do certain things as a minister of God. I do not wish to bring up these examples, lest I stir up controversies in your mind. However, I can assure you that using the logic of Jesus, you will know what is right and what will set you free. Do not be bound by tradition that do not follow the most basic laws of common sense, fairness and logic. Jesus often addressed our hypocrisy with simple logical questions. "Is it lawful to do well on the Sabbath day?" (Luke 14:3)

How much then is a man better than a sheep? Wherefore it is lawful to do well on the sabbath days.

Matthew 12:12

Indeed, it is lawful to do well on the Sabbath day. Today, we may not have a big question about the Sabbath day. There are many other things that Christians reject because of similar hypocritical sentiments. It is time for you to apply yourself, using Jesus' wisdom, "Is it lawful to do well on the Sabbath day?"

Indeed, you must do what is right, what is holy, what is moral, what is biblical, all the time. Let the Holy Spirit guide you away from traditions that have negative feedback and destroy the purpose for which they were given.

Conclusion

It is my prayer that the gift of God which has been bestowed on you will be stirred up by these few words.

To the making of many books there is no end!

Be encouraged and stirred up in the mighty anointing of these last days!